# Decision Point

---

**Real-Life Ethical Dilemmas in Law Enforcement**

**2nd Edition**

# Decision
# Point

Why do good cops sometimes make bad ethical decisions? It is often because bad cops commit wrongdoing and expect their fellow officers to cover or look the other way. Aptly named, *Decision Point* contains real-life examples of ethical decision points or moments of truth that can have lasting effects on the careers of those involved and the citizens we protect and serve. Jeff Green has written an insightful and straightforward book that from the very first chapter causes the reader to critically reflect on the many confusing and ambiguous realities of the law enforcement culture and the "code of silence" mentality that wrongly permeates our profession. This book is precisely what law enforcement officers at every level need to raise their moral awareness.

~Bill O'Toole
*Executive Director*
*Northern Virginia Criminal Justice Academy*
*Assistant Chief of Police (Retired)*
*Montgomery County, Maryland*

Insightfully and realistically probing the issues of justice and morality, Green forces us to examine our innermost values and beliefs. It is then up to each of us to decide who we want to be. *Decision Point* may be the one book that changes the very way you perceive the complexities and gravity of this noble profession.

~Greg Cappetta
*Executive Director*
*FBI National Academy Associates*

*Decision Point* is an extremely important work focusing on moral decisions that continue to challenge not only the law enforcement community but nearly all professions. Dr. Green brings to light ethical dilemmas many of us in law enforcement face as we avidly strive to uphold our solemn oath to impartially enforce laws, defend civil liberties, and protect our communities and our nation. I only wish I had this book 30 years ago when I started my career in law enforcement.

~Sylvester Jones
*Assistant Director*
*United States Marshals Service*

We all strive to develop leadership within our sphere of influence. Most of us realize this begins with leadership of self. This book offers outstanding insights to help define that internal voice that guides us when no one is watching. Every scenario is one more opportunity to talk through those leadership moments where a personal leadership theme and consistent expression of core values become more important than the actual decision. Excellent work!

*~David N. Boggs*
*Chief of Police*
*Broken Arrow, Oklahoma*

I know of no other text that brings real-world challenges to the classroom with such power, effectiveness, and truth. Green writes just as he teaches and leads—listening, questioning, probing. In short, *Decision Point* asks the tough questions, assists in the decision-making process, but ultimately puts the work on you to make the critical choices that only you can.

*~Douglas B. Merel*
*FBI Supervisory Special Agent (Retired)*
*Former Chief, Ethics Program at the FBI Academy*

Dr. Green does a masterful job presenting a wide range of real-world ethical dilemmas. His presentation of these situations and their resolution moves beyond abstract ethical platitudes to show how questions of ethics often present challenges for those in a position to intervene or report. This provides the reader with a more realistic set of conditions and discussion points that will better equip aspiring and current criminal justice personnel to face ethical dilemmas head-on.

*~Joseph A. Schafer, Ph.D.*
*Professor & Chair*
*Department of Criminology & Criminal Justice, Southern Illinois University*
*Author,* Effective Leadership in Policing: Successful Traits and Habits

*Decision Point* offers a unique and powerful presentation of the types of ethical challenges law enforcement officers confront every day. Based on actual no-win scenarios, these stories and their real-life outcomes demonstrate the difficulties of ethical decision-making and their often career-changing implications. By not providing "right" answers to these scenarios, Green helps readers understand that in the real world, these decisions can only be made by the man in the mirror.

*~Captain R. Allen Brandon*
*Uniform and Field Services Division*
*York County Sheriff's Office*
*South Carolina*

# Decision Point

---

## Real-Life Ethical Dilemmas in Law Enforcement

### 2nd Edition

Jeffrey L. Green, PhD

Glocal Press
Williamsburg, Virginia

ISBN: 978-0-9817-1162-1


Published by:
Glocal Press
Williamsburg, Virginia
Contact: info@glocalpress.com


Library of Congress Control Number: 2012954881

*The most important human endeavor is the striving for morality in our actions. Our inner balance and even our very existence depend on it. Only morality in our actions can give beauty and dignity to life.*

~Albert Einstein

# Contents

*Foreword*                                                          *xi*
*Preface*                                                           *xiii*
*Acknowledgments*                                                   *xv*

CHAPTER  1  INTRODUCTION                                             1
CHAPTER  2  OVERVIEW OF ETHICAL THEORY                              5

## Part I   Loyalty & Duty                                         17

CHAPTER  3  THE BLUE WALL                                           19
CHAPTER  4  IF NOT ME, THEN WHO?                                    27
CHAPTER  5  I'LL SEE YOU TONIGHT!                                   35

## Part II   Diversity & Discrimination                            43

CHAPTER  6  COLOR OF THE BADGE                                      45
CHAPTER  7  THE MINISTER'S MISFORTUNE                               53
CHAPTER  8  WHERE'S THE ROI AT HIS AGE?                             59

## Part III   Gifts & Gratuities                                   67

CHAPTER  9   WHERE'S THE HARM?                                      69
CHAPTER  10  PLAINCLOTHES DINNER                                    75
CHAPTER  11  ONE YEAR FROM RETIREMENT                               81

## Part IV   Use of Force                                          89

CHAPTER  12  ONE EXTRA HIT                                          91
CHAPTER  13  LOOSEN THOSE CUFFS                                     97
CHAPTER  14  DARK JUSTICE                                           103

# Part V     Search & Seizure     111

CHAPTER    15   FOUR TWENTY DOLLAR ROCKS     113
CHAPTER    16   K-9 PROBABLE CAUSE     121
CHAPTER    17   ONE BLACK HAIR     129

# Part VI     Self-Reporting     137

CHAPTER    18   THE DAY PLANNER     139
CHAPTER    19   KARMA     145
CHAPTER    20   MONSTERS AMONG US     151

# Part VII     Maintaining Confidences     159

CHAPTER    21   THE STARFISH     161
CHAPTER    22   DON'T JUDGE ME     169
CHAPTER    23   SOMETHING YOU SHOULD KNOW     177

# Part VIII     Discretion     185

CHAPTER    24   THROUGH THE EYES OF A CHILD     189
CHAPTER    25   THE TURNPIKE     195
CHAPTER    26   HOME LIFE     201

# Part IX     Informants     207

CHAPTER    27   BRING YOUR TOOTHBRUSH     211
CHAPTER    28   THE CONFIDENTIAL &     217
                (Un)RELIABLE INFORMANT
CHAPTER    29   DON'T SEARCH HIM TOO CLOSE     225

*Afterword*     231
*Sources*     235
*About the Author*     237

# Foreword

One of the greatest strengths of the U.S. justice system is that our police agencies are directly responsible to local elected officials. Many parts of the world have only large national agencies controlled by the federal government. In the United States, 800,000 police officers work in over 17,500 distinct, autonomous agencies.

The reason for this structure is that many of those who immigrated to America over the years were fleeing oppression enforced by a national police organization. As a result, these immigrants and their descendants wanted to ensure as much as possible that the police were honest, apolitical, and responsive to the needs of the average citizen.

This American system has been largely successful. Indeed, efforts to duplicate many of our strategies and policies can be seen around the world. Yet, despite the best efforts of talented police executives, periodic incidents of corruption and abuse of force and authority continue.

Numerous improvements have been accomplished over the years to address this challenge. Today candidates who want to enter law enforcement face intense competition. They are often college graduates who also served in our voluntary armed services. Candidates must score well on entrance exams, pass physical agility tests, undergo polygraph tests, and pass psychological evaluations and rigorous background investigations. This stringent selection process is undoubtedly a major reason that law enforcement is recognized as such a highly respected profession in virtually every public poll.

Despite these efforts, some police officers still commit crimes, abuse citizens, or use excessive and unjustified force. Although these instances tend to be the actions of an individual officer or a small group, we also see cases of sporadic systemic corruption that includes command staff.

As devastating as these acts of corruption and illegality can be to an agency and community, they still represent an extremely small fraction of the hundreds of thousands of honorable law enforcement officers in America. Much more prevelant and impactful are the smaller ethical decisions officers face every day – those situations in which doing the right thing is not only difficult to do but even difficult to determine.

Jeff Green's *Decision Point* is the next step in addressing these challenges. This book assists readers in understanding the real-life dilemmas law enforcement officers confront throughout their careers. The scenarios are riveting, and the discussion points force readers to consider the myriad options officers face in these dilemmas. Having worked or supervised in virtually every possible assignment, I actually can picture the individuals struggling with these complex moral decisions. One thing is certain as made clear by the decision points in every chapter—ethical decision-making is an extraordinarily difficult endeavor in the law enforcement profession.

*Decision Point* focuses on the individual officer in the middle of each situation, while making it clear that the broader culture and traditions of the agency play a major role in helping the officer make the right decision. This text therefore provides value to a wide audience, including those in entry level through supervisory and management level training programs. On many levels, Jeff Green's text is a major contribution to the policing profession.

Reading this book reminded me of a powerful quote from one of our founding fathers, Noah Webster: "The virtues of men are of far more consequence to society than their abilities." Not much has changed in 235 years.

Tom Constantine
*Superintendent, New York State Police, 1986–1994*
*Administrator, U.S. Drug Enforcement Administration, 1994–1999*
*Oversight Commissioner for Police Reform in Northern Ireland, 2000–2004*

# Preface

There are no greater occupations than those involving sacrifice in the service to others. Protecting our communities and, in doing so, our society, law enforcement may be the greatest service of all. At the core of the many challenges facing society, if we are not safe, all else fails to matter. It is with this sentiment that Winston Churchill's words to the House of Commons in World War II ring just as true today of the officers, deputies, troopers, and agents who sacrifice to keep us safe. "Never in the field of human conflict was so much owed by so many to so few."

Policing requires mental fortitude, emotional intelligence, interpersonal skills, perseverance, and many other important attributes. Yet the most important quality is character. Officers must continuously strive to develop an inner moral compass to navigate the complex ethical challenges they face throughout their daily service. Laws, codes of ethics, standards of conduct, policies, and an assortment of other ethical rules and guidelines might assist these officers. Yet at the crucible *decision point* of every ethical dilemma, the officer, alone, has to choose his own path.

> *The shaping of an ethical philosophy does not depend on recognizing and avoiding those dilemmas most often sensationalized by the media and the public. Rather, an ethical philosophy is shaped by the way an officer deals with the confusion, ambiguity, and compromise that insinuate themselves into the behavior and decisions confronting police officers every day.*
>
> ~ Joycelyn M. Pollock & Ronald F. Becker

# Acknowledgments

Writing a book takes a great deal of hard work and effort from many different people, particularly a book discussing sensitive and private moral issues. I first want to thank my wife and children. Every story, every twist, every effort to protect the trust and anonymity of the real participants, and, of course, every chapter was vetted with my family over dinners, at the soccer field, on weekends, and in the evenings, even through e-mail with my son in college. Thank you Kathy, Alexandra, and Justin for all of your guidance, enthusiasm, and unyielding support.

I am hugely indebted to many trusted friends and colleagues who provided guidance, insights, and much-needed criticism throughout this journey, particularly Ken Kilbride, a retired police lieutenant with 28 years in local law enforcement; and Paul Bertrand, a supervisory special agent with 17 years in the FBI and 8 years as a naval flight officer.

I also would like to thank the many prominent members of the criminal justice community around the world who took the time to review *Decision Point* and offer their endorsements for the cover and inside pages. I also owe a particular debt and gratitude to Thomas Constantine for evaluating the manuscript and taking the time to author such an eloquent and powerful foreword.

Finally, I want to thank the countless students—the brave men and women of law enforcement—who have shared so many personal dilemmas with me over the years. Their stories and the trials and tribulations of their decisions continue to teach and inspire me today.

# 1

# Introduction

The purpose of this text is to expose the reader to the multifaceted components of real-life ethical dilemmas thus providing opportunities to wrestle with these moral issues and better prepare for a future in this field. Studying ethical theory assists each of us frame our decisions and strengthen our moral decision-making skills. Acknowledging the role and importance of theory, *Decision Point* begins by addressing the prominent theoretical underpinnings of ethical behavior. However, the sole study of theory offers law enforcement students only modest value considering the profound practical implications of ethics in policing. John Schafer further explains this gap between classroom and real-life learning:

> *Contrived scenarios in the classroom differ significantly from real-life ethical dilemmas. In the classroom, detached participants review facts, calmly discuss options, and provide idealized solutions that neatly fit a prescribed code of ethics. Choosing the right answer in an artificial setting requires little effort. On the other hand, making the right decision in real life demands strength of character because the reality of circumstances often blurs the line between right and wrong.*

It is this gap in many police academies and university settings that *Decision Point* attempts to fill with scenarios based on real-life events and the considerations and consequences that informed the actual decisions that were made.

1

# What This Book Is Not

In preparing to write this book, I spent considerable time reflecting on personal experiences as well as sifting through those of others I knew from many years in law enforcement. It became evident very early in the process what I did *not* want *Decision Point* to be.

- As you read the stories, you will quickly realize that *Decision Point* is not about organizational ethics. Each scenario represents individual dilemmas requiring individual decisions.
- Scenarios and issues so big that they would skew the individual focus of the text were not included (e.g., the ethical implications of the USA PATRIOT Act).
- The text does not address many legally accepted practices that may have an ethical dimension (undercover operations, court-ordered eavesdropping, sting operations).
- *Decision Point* does not include dilemmas that have been covered at length in the existing literature (e.g., accepting free cups of coffee). Although such challenges are deeply important, I wanted to focus the book on slightly less charted territory. Even though the broad categories in the book have been discussed in other texts, *Decision Point* explores novel aspects of these themes.
- Finally, *Decision Point* does not include scenarios that demonstrate blatant corruption in which the correct decisions are clear.

# What This Book Is

Early on, I established five overarching criteria required of each scenario - criteria that make this book uniquely valuable.

- The stories must be based on ethical dilemmas that actually happened. The names and settings are changed in significant ways to ensure anonymity, but each scenario is based on real-life situations.

- The scenarios must have application and significance beyond their specific context.
- The stories must offer real-world value for everyone from the young student considering a career in law enforcement to the most seasoned police officer.
- The scenarios must be of a nature to most certainly cause discourse and discord in the classroom. There is no greater way to learn than in civil but spirited debate.
- The scenarios must meet the following definition of an ethical dilemma—*a situation involving a moral right or wrong where the decision is both complex and uncertain, and the decider cannot surface unscathed.*

## Final Thoughts

This brings me to the final intention of this book. You have to make the tough decisions yourself. *Decision Point* presents the scenario until the crucible moment, when the decision maker (you) has to make a choice. Because decision-making requires critical examination of the context and potential consequences (intended and unintended), each story is followed by questions and considerations to ponder before you discover the real-life choices that were made. Each chapter concludes with discussion questions for you, as an individual or as part of a group or class, to reflect on.

At no point does the text offer the "correct" course of action. Undoubtedly, many of these scenarios have correct answers pursuant to agency policies and accepted

> *The mission of policing can safely be entrusted only to those who grasp what is morally important and who respect integrity. Without this kind of personal character in police, no set of codes, rules, or laws can safeguard that mission from the ravages of police misconduct.*
>
> ~Edwin Delattre

3

standards of conduct. However, the very nature of policework is highly subjective, often executed with minimal oversight, and employed with society's tacit approval to use considerable discretion. Quite simply, rules and standards of conduct do not have the power to control the awesome responsibility officers have in the performance of their duties each day.

Developing a personal moral compass is a necessity of this sacred profession. I know most of you reading this book are considering a future in law enforcement or are already well into this noble career. I know the vast majority of you already possess a strong moral foundation. Yet deciding which right to follow or choosing between two less-than-desirable alternatives can be difficult even for the most righteous among us. I hope reading these scenarios, reflecting on the multitude of contextual considerations and real-life decisions that were made, and discussing these challenges with your peers will assist in this life-long journey.

# 2
# Overview of
# Ethical Theory

Ethics is a branch of study that focuses on the complex issues of right and wrong, responsibility, character and values, and duty. It provides a framework for how we should live together. Members of society have a duty to both self and others to maintain certain standards of behavior. Statutes and laws, which ostensibly derive from these standards, can never fully determine all challenges of right or wrong.

While the specific study of ethics is a relatively new phenomenon, philosophers have proposed different theories about the nature of morality as far back as Plato and Aristotle. The word *ethics* has its roots in the Greek word *ethos*, which translates to customs, conduct, or character. Ethical theory provides a system of principles that helps guide individuals to make decisions about what is good or bad and right or wrong.

Generally, ethical theories are divided into two categories: Teleology (from the Greek word *telos* meaning 'ends' or 'purposes') and Deontology (from the Greek word *deos* meaning 'duty'). Both of these umbrella ethical systems look at the conduct of the player with regard to the act. A third ethical category is increasingly becoming part of the ethics dialogue – Virtue-Based Ethics or the Ethics of Virtue. In contrast to a focus on the conduct of the player, virtue-based ethics emphasizes the virtues or moral character of the player.

With teleological (consequentialist) theories, the morally right decision is the one that produces good or desirable results. The focus is on the consequence of the action. With deontological theories, the morally right decision stands on its own without regard for the consequences of the decision. The rightness or wrongness of an action is intrinsic to the act itself. Deontological ethics also are referred to as rule, duty, or obligation-based ethics.

The following diagram illustrates one view of the most prominent approaches to the study of ethics.

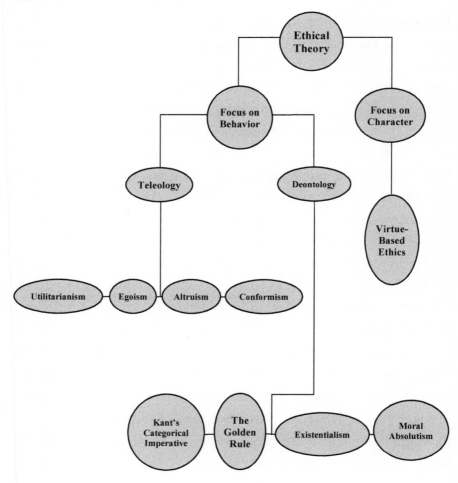

# Teleological Theory

## *Utilitarianism*

The proper decision when faced with an ethical choice is the one that either maximizes happiness or reduces suffering to the greatest possible extent for the greatest amount of people. Jeremy Bentham (1748-1832), a major advocate of this ethical approach, argued the morality of an act should be decided based on the extent to which that act contributes to the good of the majority. Hedonism, the belief that pleasure is the only intrinsic good, may be viewed as the extreme of the utilitarian approach.

This 'greatest good for the greatest number' approach has been the subject of much debate as to whether or not the ends justify the means. Thus, the most serious concern with this ethical approach is that it allows violations of very basic human values. For example, officers arrest a known terrorist who admits to having placed large explosive devices throughout the city set to detonate in one hour. Refusing to provide the location of the devices, the officers would be morally justified to torture the suspect in an effort to learn the whereabouts of the explosives. Utilitarianism would even allow the punishment of an innocent person. Under this ethical approach, the officers would be morally justified in torturing the terrorist's family.

## *Ethical Egoism*

The proper decision when faced with an ethical judgment is the one that is in the decision maker's own self-interest. The choosing of a course of action that would be the most beneficial to self does not imply that it is not favorable, or is even harmful, to others, only that the consequence to others is irrelevant when making the decision. The concerns with egoism are apparent. Most members of society would agree that the values we hold most dear would not be able to thrive if everyone was only concerned with self.

## *Altruism*

The proper decision when confronted with a moral choice is the one that helps others even if that means sacrificing one's own interests. Altruism does not imply that the decision must be harmful to self. Self, simply, is not a consideration. Coined in the 19th century by Auguste Comte, altruism is the converse of egoism.

A concern with this approach is that it does not consider the context or the primacy of the action. Consider the police officer on his way to court. He sees an elderly motorist on the side of the road with a flat tire. Even though the judge hearing his cases today consistently dismisses cases when officers do not show up for court, the officer would still have to stop and assist the motorist under altruistic ethics as this approach gives no consideration to his needs or those of society.

## *Conformism*

The proper decision when faced with an ethical choice is the one that would conform to the principles and values of the decision maker's primary social group. The concept of peer pressure plays an important role in conformist decision-making. Conformity is often associated with adolescence but clearly affects humans of all ages.

A primary concern with this approach is that it does not consider the 'rightness' of the group's decision or the values of affected individuals or other groups. Violating the law within a corrupt vice unit would be okay because the group approves of this behavior. Of course, conformism has its supporters as well. One might suggest groups such as the church, volunteer associations, or athletic groups serve as a positive form of conformism. The peer pressure and social expectations within that group lead to positive behavior consistent with the norm and values of society.

# Deontological Theory

## *Kant's Ethical Philosophy*

Immanuel Kant (1724-1804) believed that a morally correct action is performed from duty alone not from personal desires. Kant's Categorical Imperative suggests people should choose to act in a way they wish would become universal law. The proper decision is the one that, given the same circumstances, could be made into a rule for all others to follow. If it is okay for me to do it, it has to be okay for everyone to do it. If it is not okay for everyone to do it, then it is not okay for me to do it. Kant's ethical philosophy is absolute; it is *categorical*.

Kant's premise begins with the concept that the only thing good without qualification is a 'good will.' A 'good will' is one that acts in accordance with rationally determined duty. No character trait (virtue-based ethics) or consequence (teleology) is good in itself. The emphasis of the categorical imperative is that people should be treated with dignity (as ends in themselves) and never used as means towards an end. The basic view of the categorical imperative is the formation of a value-embedded foundation with the appreciation that from good intention and good will come moral judgment (Torres, 2015).

Detractors of Kant's philosophy suggest it makes no sense not to consider the consequences of one's actions. Kant's deontological approach would allow for the most horrific of outcomes as long as the action was right in and of itself. Consider the absolute nature of 'never tell a lie.' Under the categorical imperative, narcotics officers would not be able to set up sting operations; agents would not be able to pose as children on the Internet to catch pedophiles; and all undercover assignments would cease.

Supporters of Kant's philosophy speak to the power of this approach in emphasizing the moral significance of essential components of humanity such as respect, dignity, and individual rights. Consider the

Good Samaritan laws in many states. If an officer tries to assist a citizen in medical need but instead causes further injury, he is protected from liability. Society cannot, in good faith, blame the officer as long as his intervention was reasonable and within his training. According to Kantian ethics, assuming that he meant well, his good intention must count, morally speaking. If the negative outcome could not have been reasonably predicted, the fact that the outcome was positive or negative has no relevance.

### *The Golden Rule*

Although most people recognize the Golden Rule from its Christian origins in the Book of Matthew, the history of moral reciprocity predates the birth of Jesus. Reciprocity was expressed as a maxim to guide any conventional system of ethics - either in its negative form by Confucius and Buddhist and Hindu scholars or in its positive form as proclaimed by Aristotle.

- Confucianism offers, "Do not unto others what you would not have them do unto you" (Analects, 15:23).
- Buddhism holds, "Hurt not others in ways that you yourself would find hurtful" (Udana-Varga, 5:18).
- Hinduism proclaims, "This is the sum of duty: Do naught unto others which would cause you pain if done to you" (Mahabharata, 5:1517).
- In the Christian faith, Matthew 7:12 of the Bible states, "Therefore, whatever you want men to do to you, do also to them, for this is the Law and the Prophets." The Book of Matthew continues in 22:39, "You shall love your neighbor as yourself." Luke 6:31 further offers, "And just as you want men to do to you, you also do to them likewise."
- Islam requires, "No one of you is a believer until he desires for his brother that which he desires for himself" (Sunnah).

There are problems with a literal interpretation of the Rule. What if your beliefs and values are inconsistent with those of the other person? I like chocolate ice cream, and you like vanilla ice cream. The Golden Rule would require me to give you chocolate ice cream. "Do unto others as you would have them do unto you." What if the decision is agreeable to both of you but contrary to society's interests? Both of us enjoy using and selling illegal drugs. Regardless of the happy times between us, illegal drug use is not in the best interest of society. Morality requires considering the perspective of others and how one's actions affect them. Perhaps this is the real value of the Golden Rule in that it highlights this requirement.

### *Existentialism*

Existential philosophy holds that it is the individual, not societal norms or religions, who give meaning to life. People, through their own individual consciousness, create their own principles and values. They use these principles and values to find meaning in their life. Following this, it is the individual and their own understandings or right and wrong that guide ethical decisions. Existentialism stresses that individuals are fully accountable for not only what they are but also what they will be. Existentialist ethics would suggest the proper decision when faced with an ethical dilemma is the one that follows the decision maker's individual "inner voice" of right and wrong. A concern with existentialism is that it does not possess a specific code of ethics. Morality is individual. This approach gives individuals the freedom to be right or wrong with no consideration of other individuals or social norms.

### *Moral Absolutism*

Moral absolutism is the belief that certain actions are absolutely right and wrong, regardless of the intentions of the person taking them, or the consequences of the action. It is the belief certain principles exist that should not be violated. Divine Command is an example of a moral absolutist theory in that it holds morally correct actions are those that conform to the commandments of the religious person's chosen deity. Following this theory, the proper course of action when faced with an ethical decision is the one that would follow God's commandments.

This ethical approach shares the same criticism as Kantian ethics – the very nature of absolutes. For morals to be strictly absolute, they would have to be universally unquestioned and interpreted. How would we as a society ever determine what morals are absolute? All morals are all subject to individual analysis and interpretation suggesting even if absolute morals do exist, society will never be able completely agree on what those morals are.

## Virtue-Based Theories

Whereas teleological and deontological theories represent the two most notable ethical systems, there is a third approach. Contrary to the consequentialist and deontologist approach, that evaluates the actions of the player, virtue-based ethics approach the discussion from the perspective of the player's character and personal values.

The virtue-based approach also emphasizes the importance of moral

> *It is a matter of real importance whether our early education confirms in us one set of habits or another. It would be nearer the truth to say that it makes a very great difference indeed, in fact all the difference in the world.*
> ~ Aristotle

education. Virtuous behavior is a skill that can be learned. People can learn to be moral from their experiences and influences throughout their lives. "In essence, virtue-based ethics is about being and becoming a good, worthy human being" (Northouse, 2013, p. 427.) We are creatures of habit, and habits can be formed and unformed through learning and action.

A primary criticism of virtue-based ethics is that it does not provide clear guidance on *how* to act in the presence of a moral dilemma. The lack of moral rules is the main concern, but also problematic is the ambivalence to the primacy of one virtue over the other. When virtues are in conflict, which one should prevail?

Advocates would offer that this approach asks a much more relevant question - What sort of person should I be? We should strive for values such as honesty, integrity, fairness, and benevolence rather than look for absolute rules. Would you rather your leader 'always tell the truth' or 'always act with honesty and integrity?' The distinction is subtle but powerful.

## Definition of Key Terms in the Discussion of Ethics

**Applied Ethics:** The study of right and wrong pertaining to a particular profession.

**Authenticity:** Genuine, candid, sincere approach with self and others.

**Character:** The sum of all the qualities that make a person as demonstrated through values, thoughts, words, and deeds.

**Commitment:** An agreement, promise, or dedication to a person or cause.

**Confidentiality:** The duty to respect the privacy of information concerning others.

**Consistency:** Given the same situation, the action or decision should be constant.

**Courage:** Choosing to make the 'right' decision even in the face of sacrifice or personal loss.

**Corruption:** The misuse of public authority for private gain.

**Culture:** The norms and customs of a group.

**Ethical Differences:** Events in which rational players with consistent values disagree as to the outcome or choice to be made.

**Ethical Dilemma:** A situation involving a moral right or wrong where the decision is both complex and uncertain, and the decider cannot surface unscathed.

**Equality:** The responsibility to view and treat all people as moral equals.

**Impartiality:** The player should forgo personal bias to the extent possible with regard to treating one person differently from another absent a valid reason to do so.

**Intimidation:** To threaten a person in order to influence the decision or conduct…may include physical, emotional, or psychological harm.

**Misconduct:**  Violations of agency policies or procedures.

**Morals:** A sense of right and wrong based on an individual's values, beliefs, attitudes, and experiences.

**Rationality:** All legitimate moral acts must be supportable by generally accepted ethical principles.

**Values:**  The principles that we decide personally or as a society to be of importance and worth. Values strongly influence our decision-making and help determine how we interact with one another.

**Veracity:** The obligation to speak the truth.

## Moving Forward in the Text

A critical step in debating any ethical controversy is to reveal the fundamental moral principles that shape our positions. The study of *theoretical* ethics begins this process. Yet, theories are much easier to describe in a textbook than actually apply in real life. Moreover, no single theory is sufficient in providing a clear ethical basis for all moral decision-making. This clearly is evident in the complex and dynamic law enforcement profession. As we progress in the text, the focus will shift to *applied* ethics, which moves from the abstract to real-life by addressing actual moral dilemmas confronting the law enforcement community today. As you wrestle with the best resolutions to the following scenarios, I encourage you to keep in mind the various ethical approaches and principles and their potential applicability to your decision-making.

# Part I

# Loyalty & Duty

Byers (2002) suggested that "unethical behavior is the result of a conscious decision making process to abuse one's authority while in a position of public trust." I think this assertion fails to recognize the moral challenges presented every day to officers who are trying to make the conscious decision to do the right thing. If ethical decision making was just about right and wrong, we would not need this text. Yet, morality is complex. It has powerful psychological and societal influences. Simply, good officers trying to do the right thing will still often find themselves with a moral dilemma.

One of the most prevalent challenges occur when ethical virtues conflict with one another. This conflict causes challenge. It is often difficult to know how to prioritize virtues. When honesty clashes with loyalty, for example, officers may find themselves in conflict. While the categories of virtue are numerous, one of the most respected virtues in the law enforcement community in loyalty.

Loyalty is a deep-rooted characteristic, indoctrinated in all officers from the academy through the field-training program and throughout their careers. It is a trait that penetrates the very culture of policing organizations that strengthens the solidarity among officers. Although loyalty is a virtue, choosing whom or what to be loyal to often causes personal and organizational moral conflict.

What happens when loyalty to a fellow officer conflicts with loyalty to the agency? Or when loyalty to the law or Constitution conflicts with a personal moral? Or when loyalty to a family member conflicts with loyalty to society?

Loyalty is clearly a complex virtue at the root of many ethical dilemmas in policing. The following stories demonstrate the moral challenges presented when virtues conflict with one another.

# 3
# The Blue Wall

*The only thing necessary for the triumph of evil is for good men to do nothing.*

~Edmund Burke

## Detective John Parker's Story

We hit the apartment just after midnight. The previous hours had been consumed with verifying the target residence with the informant, obtaining a search warrant, planning the raid, assembling the team in full tactical gear, and conducting preraid briefings.

"Clear!" yelled Tony from the master bedroom.

"Clear!" from Jim in the guest room.

This went on for a few seconds until the entire apartment was in our control. As was our practice, we brought the occupants to a single location in the apartment, where we searched them for weapons, and I explained our purpose for being there. I then assigned several detectives to start the interviews in separate locations while other detectives started the search of the apartment for cocaine, drug paraphernalia, records, weapons, and so forth.

Tony came out of the master bedroom to report observing what appeared to be several hundred small Ziploc baggies, drug scales, and a wad of cash. I yelled over to Jim to go back with Tony and start inventorying and packaging what was there.

We eventually left the house with the primary suspect in custody, a solid confession, and corroborating evidence—three eight balls of cocaine, triple beam scales, a few hundred baggies, a detailed records ledger, and $2,400 in cash.

The suspect cooperated from the start and eventually became a confidential informant. We nicknamed him Blow to avoid using his real name. The case against him went smoothly through the court system, with guilty pleas, while he worked for me, providing information that led to an additional six search warrants and numerous arrests over the next few months. There was still the issue of the $2,400, though. One civil court appearance remained.

When the judge called our case, Tony testified in three sentences that he found the $2,400 in the bedroom with the drugs. There was no opposition to the forfeiture, and the civil case was over in less than five minutes.

As I walked down the hallway of the courthouse, I heard, "Detective, Detective!" from behind me. I turned and waited for Blow to catch up.

"Detective, I need to know if you're going to hold up your end of the deal. Since all of my court appearances are over, I gave you a lot of dope dealers, and my probation officer says I can move upstate, am I finished working for you?"

"Yeah, pal, you're done. Call me if you ever want to do this again. I'll shoot you some money next time since you won't be working off charges."

"Okay, good. Look, I need to tell you something, but I'm only going to say it once. I won't repeat this to Internal Affairs or your boss or no one. But you need to know this."

"Blow, I'm walking out. What's on your mind?"

"Detective, there was $2,800 in my bedroom that night. When that other detective [Tony] just testified there was $2,400, I didn't know what to say. I mean it was all dope money, so I don't care. But look, I'm just saying—"

"Just saying what, Blow? That my friend pocketed $400? That a police detective is corrupt? What are you trying to pull here?"

"I'm not pulling anything and not accusing anyone. Just telling you there was $2,800 there, not $2,400."

You are Detective John Parker. Reflect on these questions and considerations before reading the real-life outcome.

1.  Do you report the information, to your supervisor or to the Internal Affairs Division?
2.  Do you dismiss the information as a baseless accusation?
3.  Is there some other course of action?

## Considerations

### Position and Rank

*   Tony is the senior detective on the squad, with over twenty years of service as a police officer and over ten years as a narcotics detective.
*   You have been a narcotics detective for less than a year, with seven total years of service as a police officer.
*   Tony is highly respected throughout the department and is a mentor to new narcotics detectives.
*   You were the youngest officer ever to make narcotics detective in your police department.
*   You are viewed by most as highly competent and aggressive, but many have reservations because of your overall lack of experience.

### Blow

*   Blow is an informant. He has already demonstrated a lack of loyalty and honesty through his cooperation with you in turning on his friends and fellow drug dealers.
*   Blow has never once lied to you, and everything he has said about

21

others has turned out to be accurate.

- Blow keeps meticulous records, and even more precise is the ledger he keeps in his head.
- He is unwilling to cooperate any further, but what if he changes his mind at some point and does come forward to the department about this situation?

### *Tony*

- You and Tony are friends, and your families have spent many dinners together at each other's homes. Tony has been a strong mentor to you since you joined the squad.
- Tony did have a brief opportunity in the bedroom alone when he could have taken the $400 before coming out to notify you.
- The Internal Affairs Division could know something about Tony that you don't.
- If you move forward, will Tony's reputation be irreparably harmed, even if the accusation is eventually unfounded?
- Can the accusation really ever be unfounded with certainty in everyone's minds?
- Can the accusation ever be proven? What possible evidence could be produced at this point?

### *Policy and Code of Ethics Issues*

- Does your department have policies or a code of ethics addressing your duties to report in situations like this?
- Even if policies and guidelines exist, recognize that you still have the choice to follow or disregard them.

### *Personal and Professional Consequences*

- If you go forward with this information to the department, how will that affect your career? Your reputation? Your working relationships?
- Can you live with your decision if you bring harm to an innocent officer?
- Can you live with your decision if you let a guilty officer go free?

## The Real-Life Decision

I struggled over this dilemma for several days. So many considerations and consequences raced through my head. I did not want to hurt an innocent officer. Yet I did not want to let a corrupt officer go free.

I decided to call Jim, the detective I had asked to assist Tony with the money and drugs at the apartment. "Jimmy, don't ask me why, just answer the question: Are you positive there was $2,400 in cash in Blow's room the night we hit his apartment?"

"Tony counted it right in front of me. Twice. I'm absolutely positive. Then he packaged it, stored it in the drug room at the station, and turned it over to the property section the next day. I was with Tony every step of the way."

"Okay, Jim. . . . Thanks."

"So, why are you asking? Did Tony take some of the money off the top before I went in there?"

That last question really threw me. He asked it so matter-of-factly, with no surprise in his voice. I would have thought the very idea of Tony skimming money would have shocked the conscience, but it clearly did not shock Jim. I didn't answer his question.

I was not ready to go forward to the department, but I could not let this go either. The next day, I pulled Tony into a vacant office at the station and explained the situation. I was anticipating (well, more hope than anticipation) that he would calmly deny it all and tell me that we needed to talk to the sergeant together about it. This response would have been consistent with his nature. Tony was a good guy.

I could not have been more wrong. He lit into me with full force. "Who the hell do you think you are, accusing me of stealing? I was working a beat when you were in grade school. I'm the most honest cop in this building." His tirade went on for a couple of minutes. As quick tempered as I can be, I let him vent like that for one reason. I was actually wondering if everything he was saying was true. Who was I to even entertain what a snitch said over a decorated, highly respected detective?

I did shut Tony down after a couple of minutes and forcefully told him to walk away. He left the office, but I stayed another hour, weighing every possible consideration once again. I needed closure. I had to make a decision right then.

That afternoon was the last time I spoke of that incident for over twenty-five years.

Do I think he did it? Who knows. I really have no idea and doubt we would have ever known that answer, even if I'd made a different decision that afternoon. But my gut says yes, he took the money. And while I do not know for certain if I would do things any differently today, I think I would. I still frequently second-guess that decision made over a quarter-century ago.

## Discussion Questions

1.  If Tony did take the money, would this be categorized as police corruption in your view? Would it matter to you if it was $4, $400, $4,000, or $40,000?

2.  What competing values did Detective Parker face in this ethical dilemma?

3.  What other considerations and consequences should Detective Parker have taken into account?

4.  Do you agree or disagree with the real-life decision? Why?

5.  What is the Blue Wall of Silence (aka Blue Code of Silence), and what are its implications in the criminal justice field?

# 4

# If Not Me, Then Who?

*The accomplice to the crime of corruption is frequently
our own indifference.*

~Bess Myerson

## Detective Brian Perez's Story

I was brand new to Vice. It took most officers ten to fifteen years to make detective there, but through hard work and mostly good fortune and timing, I made it in seven years. I knew I had something to prove to those guys who had been around a long time.

I arrived to work on Monday at 5:00 p.m. Within two hours, I was on an arrest team taking down a cock-fighting ring in the northeast. The following night, I hung out with detectives who were working prostitutes on the strip. We must have made a dozen arrests that evening. Wednesday, I sat by myself in a surveillance van watching a bookie's house, which the squad was planning to raid Sunday night after the football games. Thursday was court day, so the team worked day shift and took the evening off. Friday evening was about catching up with all the paperwork for the week. Two of the guys said they might have something brewing for later, but for now, everyone was typing, packaging evidence, and talking on the phone.

What a great week it had been. I felt I had learned more in the last few days than in the last few years. And these guys really knew how to treat a new guy right. Not only were they exposing me to a side of law enforcement I had never seen, but they were also treating me like one of them. Even at dinner, every night someone on the team had picked up my tab—and these guys ate well!

We were a couple of hours into Friday evening when the sergeant walked into the squad area with a big wad of cash. Everyone walked over to get some of it. I had no idea what they were doing, so I sat tight at my desk, continuing to work on a chore that Keith (one of the senior guys) had given me earlier. When the sergeant was finished with everyone, he walked over to me and threw $150 on my desk.

"Brian, this is your weekly buy money. As you've probably noticed this week, there are unplanned times when we need cash to do our job. Maybe we need to place a quick bet, or maybe we need cash to pick up a prostitute. This way, you'll always have money on you for those times."

"How do you want me to account for the money I spend? It's not like we can ask the bad guys for receipts."

"We really don't keep up with it to a penny. Get with one of the guys to see how we do it."

The sergeant walked back into his office, and a few minutes later, Keith came by to check my progress. "Hey kid, how's that financial chart going?"

"Not bad, I guess, considering it's my first stab at something like this."

"You'll get the hang of it. Tonight is your turn to buy dinner for everyone. You get to pick the place too."

"So that's why I haven't paid this week. We all take turns paying for everyone. But Keith, I can't afford to go to the places we've been going, especially paying for the entire squad."

"No, no, no. We use our buy money for it. It works out on average that each of us pays once every two weeks. We get a fresh $150 every week from the sergeant. So out of the $300 you get over a two-week period, you take about $150 or so out for dinner. That still leaves you $150 for work-related stuff for that two weeks, and if you need more, we can pool a little among us or go back to the well on bigger things."

"Are you kidding?" I practically whispered. "There is no way this could be on the up-and-up."

"We work crazy hours all the time. We give this city seven days and nights a week. Three-fourths of us are divorced because of our work schedules. Paying for our dinner is the least the city can do. Look, both the sergeant and lieutenant know about this. I've been here twelve years, Brian, and it was this way when I got promoted. It's just the way it is. It's all good."

You are Detective Brian Perez. Reflect on these questions and considerations before reading the real-life outcome.

1. Do you go along with this long-time practice on the vice squad?
2. Do you report the practice to Internal Affairs?
3. Is there some other course of action?

## Considerations

### Severity and Scope of the Practice

- It is only dinner.
- Yet those dinners every night for every member of three vice squads adds up to a considerable amount of money.
- Who else is engaged in similar practices? Narcotics squad? The street crimes unit?
- Who else is aware of this practice?
  - The entire detective division?
    - ○ Veteran patrol officers?
    - ○ Supervisors and mid-management beyond the vice squads?
    - ○ The deputy chief . . . the chief?

### Policy and Legal Issues

- The practice is not condoned by the city.
- It is a crime with significant ramifications, bilking tens of thousands of dollars out of the city, which means illegally taking money out of citizens' pockets.

### *Personal and Professional Consequences*

- If you join your peers, at some point a new detective or a new supervisor will report what's going on. Will you be around at that time, and what will be the impact on you and your family?
- If you report this practice, how will that affect you, your family, and your agency?

### *Community Impact*

- If the community finds out, how would it respond? What would this do to community/police relations?

## The Real-Life Decision

"Keith, you're sure the sergeant and lieutenant say this is okay?"

"Absolutely, as well as every other sergeant and lieutenant before them. . . . It's just the way it's done, Brian. If it was really that bad, don't you think someone would have put a stop to it by now?"

That evening was the first time I had ever stolen anything. I hardly slept a wink. You'd think it would only get easier, but not for me. It just got harder and harder. And not just when I paid, but every single night I ate out, knowing I was stealing.

One other detective, Jackson, seemed to make as many excuses not to eat out as I did. I had to know if he was suffering like me, but that was a tough conversation to start.

"Jackson, you've been up here two years. I've noticed you're not really part of the clique. You rarely attend 'choir practices' after work, and you seem to have dinner plans outside the team more than most of us. I know this is a personal question, but is the distance you keep from everyone about the buy money thing up here?"

"Brian, I don't much care for it. They all know I'm not a fan. It's flat-out wrong. Hell, it's corrupt. But they all trust me to keep my mouth shut, which is what I do. And who am I to do something about it, anyway? I just stay away from it to the extent I can."

31

"I've been up here six months. I won't last another six months with this guilt. Maybe together we can end this."

Over the next two weeks, we decided to put a stop to this corrupt practice. But choosing how to end it was difficult. We knew that confronting the guys with an ultimatum would only cause us harm. Plus, the practice crossed all three vice squads. I didn't even know those other guys that well. We knew going through our chain of command would be ineffective. At minimum, our sergeant and lieutenant already knew. The entire chain could have been in on it. After all, many of the senior executives had done time in the vice squads over the years. Our first choice was the state police. But since we had two state police special agents on our task force, we were even hesitant to do that. We decided on the FBI.

I recall distinctly the first time we met with the agents, twenty miles outside of town at an old industrial park. We told them about everything, including our nightly participation since joining the squad. Our trepidation must have been evident to the agents. One of them pulled out a calculator and started adding the meals together.

"Brian, Jackson, we know this is difficult. We carry a badge and a sense of loyalty to each other just like you do. But you're not just describing a free dinner on the city. Look at these numbers. We are looking at over a hundred thousand dollars just in a few years. If this has been occurring for years and years like you believe, that number goes up exponentially. And more important, if a culture of corruption exists throughout the vice squads, who knows what else is going on in your department? This is serious. We're going to move on this, but we need your help."

My emotions over the next few months ranged from righteousness to betrayal to fear. I second-guessed myself every day and night. Not even our wives knew that Jackson and I went to work most evenings wired with listening devices. The FBI even planted court-ordered recording devices throughout the squad areas, supervisors' and managers' offices, and briefing rooms. At one point, the highest levels of my department were under physical and electronic surveillance.

In all, thirty-eight police officers, including two captains, a major, and the deputy chief, were indicted on various corruption charges—some far beyond the free dinners. The chief retired in disgrace after thirty years on the job. Charges were dropped on four officers with the agreement that they immediately retire and forfeit their pensions. Of the remaining thirty-four officers, all pled guilty but two, who eventually lost their fights at trial.

Jackson and I are still with the department. Both of us are senior executives now, but our careers haven't been easy. Even today, new recruits look at the two of us differently. Most cops think we did the right thing, but we still wear the Scarlet letter on our foreheads.

Two questions kept me pushing through those hard times. If not me, then who? If not now, then when? I'm not sure the path we chose was exactly right, but I can still look in the mirror with a reasonable sense of honor and integrity, knowing that I had the moral courage to do the unthinkable in order to uphold my oath to the law and to the people of my community.

## Discussion Questions

1. Policing is clearly not among the highest-paying professions in the United States. This is despite its dynamic, complex, and dangerous challenges. This is despite many of its members being highly educated men and women with unscrupulous character. In your view, does relatively low pay entitle officers to certain perks, possibly even having their dinners paid for, off the record, by their agency?

2. If you think the free dinners were okay, what would tip that belief to the other side? Would it matter to you if they were pocketing $10 or $15 in cash every night instead of using that money on dinner?

3. Give this scenario some real thought. Recognizing the artificial confines of the classroom, what do you think you would have done if actually faced with this dilemma?

# 5

# I'll See You Tonight!

*Only by being moral can criminal justice be distinguished from the very crime it condemns.*

~ Jay Albanese

## Deputy Sheriff Martin Thompson's Story

I was a young cop, looking for my first place to live away from home. A federally sponsored program was announced at roll call offering low-cost housing to any law enforcement officer willing to live in specific low-income, high-crime areas. I immediately took advantage of the offer.

The next year was an adjustment. Nothing in life is free, of course, so my role, even when off duty, was to be the cop everyone came to with their issues. And they came frequently. For the most part, I didn't mind. These were by and large good people, and my existence there was important for police/community relationships.

Elisa lived several houses down from me. I had met her a few times but did not really know her. She was a single mother and kept to herself for the most part. One afternoon, as I was getting ready for my evening shift, Elisa knocked on my door.

"Officer Thompson, I . . . I need to talk to you. I need your help."

"I'm on my way to work. But if it can't wait, I can call in late."

35

"It's important, Officer. I'm very sorry."

"Give me two minutes to call work."

I phoned the roll call sergeant and explained why I would be late. No issues there.

"Elisa, what's on your mind?"

"Something happened to me today. I don't know what to do. I was driving home for lunch. About a half mile from here, an officer pulled me over because my license plates had expired. The officer also found out that I don't have a green card."

"I'm surprised he let you go. No disrespect, Elisa, but our policy is pretty strict on illegals."

"This is why I am talking to you. I had my little baby with me in the backseat. When he started talking about arresting me right there and sending me back to Mexico, all I could think about was my baby. I was crying and didn't know what to do. I begged him to let me and my baby go. He said, 'Only one way you don't go back to Mexico, . . .'" Her voice hitched. She was crying pretty hard now. "He said, 'We'll start with a blow job and go from there. And I like sex rough with my women.' Officer Thompson, I couldn't go to jail. I couldn't be deported. I told him to meet me at 9:00 tonight at that little hotel just around the corner from here."

I was skeptical, but I still tried to appear comforting. "I'm very sorry this happened to you. But you're accusing a fellow officer of a serious crime. I need you to give me exact details of the stop and the conversation, and I need to know who the officer was. And are you willing to take a polygraph this afternoon to verify that you're telling me the truth?"

"No polygraph. I'm only talking to you, no one else in your department. As for the officer, his name tag read Deputy M. Johnson."

She had just provided me the name of one of the most respected deputies in our agency. Everyone liked Johnson. He was a veteran deputy who taught in police academies throughout the state. He had been offered numerous promotions over the years but always turned them down because he liked the road. He had even been courted to run for sheriff a few years back.

"Are you positive the deputy was M. Johnson?"

"I'm sure. He was like six foot six, dark black skin like yours, and had a very deep, intimidating voice. I am so scared."

"Is there anything else he said or did that I need to know about?"

"The last thing he said was, 'You better be there tonight. And don't f--- with me either. If you don't give it up like I like it, I'll take it. And you won't like how I take it. I'll see you tonight!'"

You are Deputy Sheriff Martin Thompson. Reflect on these questions and considerations before reading the real-life outcome.

1. Do you tell Elisa to just go home, that there's nothing you can do?
2. Do you report Deputy Johnson to the department?
3. Is there some other course of action?

## Considerations

### *Position and Rank*

* Johnson is a respected veteran deputy in the department.
* You have a good reputation but are fairly new on the job.

### *Elisa*

* What are the implications if she is telling the truth?
* If she is lying?
* Does her unwillingness to take a polygraph exam or talk with anyone else in the agency affect the veracity of her story?
* If she is telling the truth, will she be in danger if you report Johnson?
* If she is telling the truth, will she be in danger if you do not report Johnson, and she does not show up at the hotel?

### *Johnson*

* If Deputy Johnson is engaged in this illegal behavior, is he involved in other illegal behavior?
* What if Johnson is completely innocent? How will reporting him affect his career? His reputation?

- Legal Issues
- If Johnson did what he is accused of doing, his action would be a state felony and violate federal laws.
- You also have Elisa's illegal immigration status to address.

***Personal and Professional Consequences***
- Of course, the final outcome will play a significant role in other people's perceptions of your decision. Based only on what you know at this point, however, how do you think your fellow officers would view you if you report Johnson to the Internal Affairs (IA) Division? If you do not report him?
- Either way, this incident will affect your career.
- Either way, this incident will be a defining moment for you.
- Can you live with yourself if you do not report and later discover that Johnson had used his badge to rape other women prior to and after Elisa's accusation?

***Community Impact***
- What if there are victims already in the community too afraid to come forward?
- Will there be additional victims in the future?
- What impact will reporting Johnson have on the community if he is innocent? If he is guilty?

## The Real-Life Decision

Deputy Johnson was a living legend in our department and in the surrounding jurisdictions, but I could not ignore this accusation. Part of me wanted to meet with him and get his side of the story, but the complaint was so egregious. What if the accusation was true? What if he had done this before to other women? What if he had done even more to other women? After all, his final comments to Elisa indicated a very violent, deviant capacity. My only concern in reporting this was if Elisa was lying. Accusations like this could ruin a good officer's reputation forever.

Elisa had appeared distraught and sounded sincere, but what about her unwillingness to cooperate with a polygraph? That bothered me. I basically had only the word of a woman I didn't even know. If I was going to act, I had to act now or walk away from this.

I called my sergeant, gave him the quick version of the accusation, and told him we needed to get IA involved. He agreed and made the call to IA himself.

Within minutes, the captain of IA called my residence and gave me a location to meet his team. I met them at a nearby warehouse and explained the accusation in detail. The captain needed to talk directly to Elisa. I called her and explained how important her cooperation was in preventing other women from abuse in the future. She reluctantly agreed to meet with both of us.

Elisa again explained the details of the traffic stop and the conversation with Deputy Johnson. The captain excused himself, walked a few feet away from us, and called the commander of the communications center to check Johnson's traffic stops. He walked back over and told us both there was no record of Johnson stopping a single vehicle today. Elisa held firm to her story, even when pressed by the IA captain.

The captain shared my concerns with going after this highly respected, highly decorated officer, particularly with no record of the traffic stop to corroborate even that part of Elisa's story. Yet her tone and demeanor appeared credible. The captain decided to move forward against Johnson, but he wanted more proof than her word against his.

The IA group met and came to the consensus that Elisa should go to the hotel as planned with Johnson. IA first established a covert surveillance perimeter around the hotel. Then they wired one of the hotel rooms with both audio and video surveillance. Because of Deputy Johnson's expertise with hand-to-hand combat and weapons prior to and during his police career, as well as his huge size and potential for violence, the captain activated a small group within the SWAT team that he had used in the past on sensitive operations.

The SWAT deputies arrived in plainclothes as instructed and positioned themselves in the adjoining room with us for an immediate entry if the situation deteriorated. Finally, Elisa was placed in the room alone with still nearly two hours to spare.

Johnson showed at the hotel at 8:50 p.m., driving his personal vehicle. He parked beside Elisa's car. Elisa waved at him from the front window of her hotel room. When he walked in the room, he was all business.

"You're looking finer now than when I stopped you. Now take your damn clothes off."

Elisa forced a small smile. "I'm gonna let you f--- me, but how do I know you won't lock me up anyway?"

"You don't need to know s---. You're going to one way or the other." Johnson was visibly agitated. "Rip your shirt off right now, or I'm going to beat the s--- out of you and rip it off myself!"

As Johnson started to move aggressively toward Elisa, the IA captain gave the order to move in. The tactical guys hit the room and took Johnson to the ground with unmitigated force. I grabbed Elisa and secured her in the safety of the adjoining room.

When the story broke in the news, other victims came forward. My involvement with the case ended with this incident, but there were other convictions with other victims. Johnson is still in prison today.

## Discussion Questions

1. What other possible concerns or consequences should have been considered in this dilemma?

2. Accusing a fellow officer, particularly a highly respected veteran, is not a path any young officer wants to choose. Yet this deputy felt the severity of the accusation outweighed the lack of evidence supporting Elisa's accusation. In hindsight, he obviously made the right decision. But do you think you would have made the same decision knowing only what you knew from Elisa? Support your choice.

# Part II
## Diversity & Discrimination

The environment in which police carry out their duties has changed significantly in recent years. Terrorism, advancing technologies, economic downturns, and the globalization of both law enforcement and criminal enterprises are just a few examples of transformational influences on the policing field. Possibly the most observable change facing police agencies today is society's growing diversity and plural affiliations.

Recognizing and valuing diversity helps develop a vibrant community capable of powerful collaboration and innovation. Yet, as pluralism offers distinct opportunities, it also presents potential conflict. Cultural diversity can be a source of tension between police and community if divergent responses to people are perceived as discrimination. Police agencies must be seen as fair, open minded, and tolerant of diversity, not only with the community but also within the agency. Justice, equality, and respect inspire public confidence.

Diversity and the discrimination that can follow reflect many areas of our society. Race, gender, age, social and economic status, sexual orientation, and religion are just a few examples where bias and ignorance can lead to unethical conduct. This section starts with a story ostensibly about race.

> *Never before have we faced such a firestorm of criticism and declining public trust. It is up to us to step up to the plate for the future of integrity in law enforcement.*
> *That integrity is gained by taking a closer look at each of our agencies and determining how best to reinforce our foundations. Diversity is a key component in this struggle for credibility.*
> ~ Jennifer Steck

# 6

# Color of the Badge

*It is never too late to give up your prejudices.*
~Henry David Thoreau

## Sergeant Trevor Bailey's Story

"Unit 902, copy—a gas drive-off at the Exxon station. . . ."

It was 11:15 p.m., and the midnight-shift officers were minutes from marking on duty from roll call. Officer Sherry Wilkins went to the service station, took the $10 larceny report, and ran the license plate the cashier had written down when the driver of an Explorer had taken off without paying. The clerk only wanted the money, believing the driver had simply forgotten to pay. Wilkins called the owner of the Explorer at home and left a message to call the Exxon station as soon as possible.

I was Officer Wilkins's sergeant. Normally, she would have brought the report to me, but since she finished it after midnight, she gave it to the midnight sergeant. Both Wilkins and I were off the following three days.

One of my fellow sergeants called me at home on day three of my break. "Hey, the lieutenant is out of his mind about Wilkins not submitting the follow-up report on that gas drive-off. Just giving you a heads up what to expect when you come in tomorrow."

The midnight sergeant had assigned the investigation back to Wilkins, not knowing she was going on break. Department policy is that all follow-up reports have to be submitted within forty-eight hours of the assignment. Thus, by now, the follow-up report was a day late.

I got to work early the next day and grabbed Wilkins before roll call. "Sherry, what happened with that gas drive-off a few days ago?"

"I don't know, Sergeant. I guess the midnight sergeant assigned it to one of his own guys since I was going on break. Regardless, the Exxon left me a voicemail a couple of days ago, saying the people in the Explorer stopped in and paid for the gas. The station doesn't want to pursue this any further."

"I'm glad the incident is cleared up, but check your box. How would the midnight sergeant know you were going on break?"

We walked over to the mailboxes, and sure enough, the assignment was there. Sherry was apologetic and assured me it would never happen again. I told her to be smart about things in this job, even the little things.

"Sergeant, am I in trouble?"

"No, we all make mistakes. Get the follow-up report submitted before hitting the road and make sure this doesn't happen again."

Just after 2:00 am, the lieutenant radioed me to meet him in the parking lot on Route 30 and Haskins Road. We pulled our vehicles alongside each other driver side to driver side with the windows down.

"Sergeant, I know you've only had your stripes for a few months, and this may be uncomfortable for you, but we have a significant problem on our hands."

"What's up, LT?"

"Do you know about the Wilkins incident?"

"I'm aware she was a day late turning in a follow-up report, a report she didn't even know was assigned to her until a few hours ago. But regardless, I've already handled that situation. So, no sir, I don't know what *significant* incident you're talking about."

"That's not significant to you?" The lieutenant started to raise his voice.

I remained calm. "Lieutenant, it was a small mistake. It's her first mistake like this. She's fairly new, and it won't happen again. It's already handled, sir."

"I want her charged with neglect of duty!"

I was absolutely mystified by this order. "I can't do that. I told her the incident was behind us. Doing that would completely undermine my authority with her and every other officer on the shift. And more important, I've never heard of any precedent in the history of the department for such a massive response to such a small incident."

"What part of lieutenant," he shouted, pointing to the bars on his collar, "and what part of sergeant," pointing to the stripes on my sleeve, "don't you understand? You will charge her!"

In the brief seconds before I responded, an overwhelming sense of what was happening hit me. This was too out of the norm to be categorized simply as poor leadership. It had to be something deeper, and I knew what it was. We were predominantly a white police department in a white area of the country with mostly white males as officers. Wilkins was a black female. She was friendly, intelligent, educated, physically and emotionally strong, and had a great way with people. She definitely had a promising career ahead of her . . . unless the lieutenant had his way.

You are Sergeant Trevor Bailey. Reflect on these questions and considerations before reading the real-life outcome.

1. Do you follow the lieutenant's direct order?
2. Do you stand your ground and refuse?
3. Is there some other course of action?

## Considerations

### *Position and Rank*

- Lieutenant obviously outranks sergeant.
- The lieutenant is an old-timer in the department and is rumored to be on the short list to make captain.
- You are still in your one-year probationary period as a sergeant. Under state law, you can be demoted without cause during this time.

### *The Lieutenant*

- How do you *know* this is race related? You have no evidence of this. It is just a hunch.
- Are you sure the lieutenant is not just a stickler for policy adherence?
- Are you sure there is no precedent for this strong of a sanction?

### *Policy Issues*

- Wilkins was in violation of department policy.
- Does department policy articulate appropriate sanctions for this offense?

- Does overall department policy or standard practice demonstrate a progressive approach to discipline?

### *Personal and Professional Consequences*

- What if you are right about the lieutenant's motive? Can you live with the decision to charge Wilkins with such a severe sanction that will undoubtedly have a negative impact on her career?
- Are you prepared to face the negative impact on your own career if you refuse?

## The Real-Life Decision

"Lieutenant, I am not charging her with neglect of duty. With all due respect, she doesn't deserve that for this type of mistake. A neglect of duty will stain her record forever."

"I said charge her!" he yelled.

"I suggest *you* charge her if you feel this strongly about it. And lieutenant . . . I will be in her corner every step of the way!"

The lieutenant slammed the gear shift into drive and sped out of the parking lot, tires squealing. I knew without a doubt I had just given up the stripes I had worked so hard to earn. I was angry and sad at the same time.

The one thing I did feel good about was that Wilkins would probably be okay. I had done the right thing and would continue to support her in the coming months, regardless of my personal fate.

Later that night, I told the senior sergeant on the shift what had happened. He said the lieutenant had already told him.

"So, you think Sherry will be okay in the long run?"

"I do. What the lieutenant wants is way over the top. You did the right thing."

"So, you think I'll still be a sergeant in six months?"

"Of course not. Scott, your stripes are gone. You disobeyed a direct order, and he's spun up like crazy. But you still did the right thing," he offered with a big grin across his face.

Weeks went by with no word on anything. I had not told Officer Wilkins about this incident. The lieutenant and I did not have the best relationship during that time, but we were professional and cordial to each other. Many times I almost asked him where things were, but I always chose to let sleeping dogs lie.

About three months after the incident in the parking lot, the senior sergeant I had talked to after the altercation with the lieutenant stopped by my house with a basketball and beer. As we started shooting hoops in the backyard, he told me he had heard some news related to the Wilkins situation. I thought, *Okay, here it is. Beer, basketball. . . . Wilkins is being charged with neglect of duty, and I'm being demoted.*

"Tomorrow morning, the chief is going to announce that the lieutenant is under federal investigation for making significant, unwanted sexual advances toward Wilkins, and the lieutenant is immediately being demoted to the rank of administrative sergeant pending the outcome of the investigation. From what I'm hearing, he'll be lucky to only get fired."

"What? Are you kidding me? Sexual advances? I thought all this was over race! It was actually because he had been trying to hook up with Sherry, and she had been turning him down?"

With the same grin he had given me that night three months ago, he replied, "Well, Scott, looks like you were right and wrong at the same time."

# Discussion Questions

1.  Do you believe an ethical dilemma actually existed for the sergeant? A potentially valid position is that since the lieutenant outranks the sergeant, the sergeant is obligated to follow the order—no questions asked. Thus, no dilemma existed.

2.  Are there situations when disobeying a direct order is appropriate:

    *   Legally?
    *   Ethically?
    *   Morally?

3.  Do you agree with Sergeant Bailey's real-life decision? Given only the information offered to the decision point, what do you think you would have done?

4.  Now that you know the outcome of the situation, does that change how you might make decisions in the future?

# 7

# The Minister's Misfortune

*Sometimes loyalty is misplaced or given to those who do not deserve it.*

~Unknown

## Investigator Ross Jennings's Story

Honestly, I loved my job, but there was one aspect of it I just hated. About once a quarter, the citizen complaints would force my vice squad to work the mall restrooms. Around lunchtime most days, gay men would frequent the bathrooms looking for anonymous sex. This problem was common across the country in malls and public parks. Besides the social problems this caused, it was illegal—either misdemeanor lewd behavior or felony solicitation to commit sodomy. Sure, sodomy was an ancient law on the books, never enforced between consenting adults in the privacy of their home, but it was a good way for us to keep sex out of the public bathrooms.

"Someone has to be the bait, guys," the sergeant barked. "We can draw straws, or one of you can volunteer." No one answered. He looked at Vinny and said with a smile, "Thanks, Vinny. You saved us the trouble of having to play games."

Vinny truly was the best at this. He had tight bicycle pants that would

53

drive the guys crazy. Vinny probably got more than his fair share of bait duty, but he did it well and was always a great sport about it.

We set up in the storage area adjacent to the bathroom wall. After we wired Vinny and told him the take-down words, "Blue Oyster," he made his entry. As soon as he walked in the door, it was like a feeding frenzy. We could hear one guy after the other making conversation with him. As the chatter slowed, we heard two doors shut and lock. Vinny was in one of the stalls, and another man was in the stall next to him.

Within a second, the man in the next stall over made first contact. "Hey, how's it going?"

"Doing great," Vinny replied. "Just been a little bored today."

"Well, maybe I can help with that," the man eagerly offered.

They went through a little more small talk. Many of the people we arrested in the bathrooms had criminal histories for this behavior. They knew certain key words and actions to avoid as well as key phrases to hear in return. The ones who had done this for years played the game well. This was certainly not the first time this guy had done this.

"What do you like?" he asked. This last question meant the games were nearing an end, and the man was feeling confident about Vinny.

"I like to receive more than anything," Vinny said softly.

"You're not a cop, are you?" It's funny how so many people, even those who have been arrested before, think a police officer cannot lie about that question.

"If I was a cop, would I be in here trying to hook up with you? Of course I'm not a cop."

"I believe you. . . . Hold on just a minute." Within seconds, Vinny was yelling, "Blue Oyster, Blue Oyster, Blue Oyster!" We ran into the bathroom, kicked the doors to both stalls, and there it was. Vinny's new acquaintance had taken advantage of the hole in the partition between the stalls and inserted *himself* for Vinny's pleasure. Vinny was surprised but clearly not amused.

We arrested the guy and brought him down to the mall security office. It was not an easy arrest either. As many men do in this situation, he put up a good fight. He explained in the office that he was married with children and held a position of respect in the community. This was also not uncommon.

I checked his information through Dispatch—criminal history and such. Within just a couple of minutes, my cell phone rang.

"Investigator Jennings, this is Unit 16." It was the captain in charge of the communications center. "Why is Vice running this man's information?"

"Captain, we're up at the mall and, well, you know what we do up here from time to time. We've got him on felony solicitation."

"Bullshit! You guys don't have an f---ing clue what you're doing!" he yelled. "You're all out of control!"

"Captain, you may want to call my captain. I think he's at headquarters right now. I need to go."

"Hold on. Hold on. I'm sorry. Are you absolutely sure you're right about this?" he asked, clearly trying to force himself to calm down.

"Without a doubt. It's all on tape too. And just so you know, this isn't his first rodeo either."

"Jennings, . . . he's my minister. He has over a thousand people in his congregation. I'm a deacon in his church. I need to look out for him and the church. I know you understand. Please don't do this to this man. Don't do this to our church community."

You are Investigator Ross Jennings. Reflect on these questions and considerations before reading the real-life outcome.

1. Are you swayed by the captain's plea?
2. Do you stand your ground and continue with the arrest?
3. Is there some other course of action?

## Considerations

### *The Captain*

- The captain is a good guy with a reputation for being an honest cop who looks out for his officers and the public.
- He clearly outranks you several times over and is part of the department's executive command staff.
- The captain appears to be motivated by a sense of loyalty to his church and community, not by personal gain or self-preservation.

### *Competing Values*

- The preservation of the minister's church community may be in conflict with the welfare of the greater community.
- Loyalty to your captain may be in conflict with loyalty to the law and to the community.

### *Nature of the Crime*

- The behavior was ostensibly between two consenting adults.
- The behavior was in a public restroom.
- You have no ill will toward homosexual men, but the idea of two men having sex goes against your personal values and upbringing.

## The Real-Life Decision

"Captain, I am very sorry this has happened to you and your church. I promise you my team will be as discreet as humanly possible throughout the entire booking process. But he is already in custody, we already have a statement from him, and we will be transporting him to the magistrate's office shortly. Please feel free to meet us there."

The captain replied, "I don't understand why you can't exercise a little discretion here. I bet if this was one of your drug mopes you would let this go in a second, especially if he was willing to flip on other drug dealers. And Jennings, just so you know, the idea of homosexuality bothers me more than most people. But c'mon, is that really any of the police department's business?"

"Sir, if there's anything else we can do for you throughout this ordeal, please let me know. We'll be at the magistrate's office in a few minutes."

## Discussion Questions

1.  Does the behavior of the minister in the public restroom really represent a problem to society, or is it a victimless crime between two consenting adults?

2.  Would your feelings change if the behavior was heterosexual instead of homosexual?

3.  What are the potential consequences of covering up this incident?

4.  What are the potential consequences of moving forward with the charges despite the captain's plea?

5.  Case law surrounding the Fourth Amendment speaks to the concept of *community standards* in the context of applying search and seizure to practice. Do you think community values and norms are important in enforcing laws such as this?

# 8

# Where's the ROI at His Age?

*The essence of age is intellect.*
*Wherever that appears, we call it old.*
~ Ralph Waldo Emerson

## Agent Dale Gibson's Story

I was on a promotion board to fill a senior management position, and at first it was pretty routine except for the unusually high number of applicants. All the voting members on the board were senior managers. The chair was a senior executive with no vote absent a dispute that could not be settled otherwise. The secretary of the board, also a nonvoting member, was the lowest in rank as well as the minority representative required by policy.

Over the past two weeks, each of us had painstakingly reviewed several months' worth of supervisor evaluations, test scores, interviews, and, of course, each candidate's application package, articulating the applicant's training, education, and experience. Through a blind process, we had narrowed the final list to ten candidates. Today's purpose was to rank the five best candidates in descending order for recommendation to Human Resources for selection.

The chair discussed the rules and processes we would follow that day. We began the promotion board by giving each voting member an opportunity to highlight the strengths and weaknesses of each candidate. When this process was complete for all ten candidates, the chair opened the meeting for a general discussion of where each person should be ranked. For some reason, we started with who should not be ranked. We were able to agree rather quickly on those five candidates. We then moved to number five, then four, and then three. Two superb candidates remained. We spent quite a while rediscussing their strengths and weaknesses. What we were left with was that either candidate would have been an exceptional choice for the number-one ranking.

Then one of the board members commented, "We could let age be the decider."

"What do you mean, Jerry?" I asked. "Both have plenty of experience to be successful."

"I'm not talking about youth. One is several years older than the other and is already eligible to retire. Think about it. Where's the ROI at his age?"

I was no policy guru, but I felt pretty confident that talking about age and return on investment (ROI) in the same breath was a taboo area in the realm of age discrimination. More important, this applicant was stellar. How could we use something like age against him? He was only fifty-two!

I decided to speak up. "I really think we have to take age off the table. I'm not convinced age is the only way to separate these candidates, and I'm pretty sure it's against policy."

Jerry did not raise his voice, but he did become a little animated. "Why, Dale?" he asked as he looked around the table. "I'm just being honest. And regardless of policy, this board is private. What we discuss and why we make our decisions do not leave this room."

Everyone looked toward the chair for his opinion. He looked around the room a few seconds before commenting. "Folks, all things being equal here, I think the age argument is valid. He could retire tomorrow after we spent months on this selection. We'll rank the younger candidate number one. This concludes this promotion board."

You are Agent Dale Gibson. Reflect on these questions and considerations before reading the real-life outcome.

1. Do you remain silent?
2. Do you argue your position even after the chair has concluded the selection board?
3. Do you report the incident (e.g., chain of command, EEO office)?
4. Is there another course of action?

## Considerations

### *Legal and Policy Issues*

- What does your agency policy say about age discrimination? What about the law?
- Does the policy or law apply in this situation?

### *Competing Values*

- Do you show loyalty to the chair (senior in rank), or do you show loyalty to the affected candidate?
- What would loyalty to the organization or even the community require of you in this situation?
- Even if policy or law does not apply to the chair's decision, is this a case of discrimination in your eyes?
- Exposing the incident would violate the sensitive and private nature of the promotion board. Not exposing the incident may violate the rights of the affected candidate.

### *Personal and Professional Consequences*

- Taking an adamant stand after the board was concluded may adversely affect your reputation with the chair and your peers.
- Reporting the matter outside the board may have negative implications, as some may see you as disloyal.
- Reporting the matter outside the board may have positive implications, as some may see you as a stand-up person.

## The Real-Life Decision

I didn't sleep too well that night. I kept going over the pros and cons of the board's decision. The age argument did have some merit. I would hate to promote this guy only for him to retire in three months. On the other hand, he had given the organization almost twenty-five years of his life and was well deserving of this promotion. And just because he was eligible to retire certainly did not mean he would retire anytime soon. Then there was the legal issue. I didn't know for sure, but I thought age was a protected EEO status.

The next morning I called Human Resources and asked a hypothetical question. Could age be used as a factor in promotions? The HR representative read me the following law, directly from the U.S. Equal Employment Opportunity Commission (EEOC):

> *Under the laws enforced by EEOC, it is illegal to discriminate against someone (applicant or employee) because of that person's race, color, religion, sex (including pregnancy), national origin, age (40 or older), disability or genetic information.*

I hung up the phone and sought out a trusted friend, who was the same rank as I was and had been around quite a while. "Any advice on what I should do?

He smiled. "Dale, you wouldn't have told me any of this if you'd planned on keeping it to yourself. Sounds like you've already made the right decision without my help."

I went to the chair of the board to make my case one last time. I told him what the EEOC law was, and that he or I had to make this situation right. My not-so-subtle threat was not lost with him. He was visibly upset with me for questioning his authority, but he kept his composure.

"The paperwork has already been submitted to HR. What exactly do you expect me to do at this point?" he asked.

"My suggestion is that you call HR, pull the paperwork based on an honest mistake made by the board, and then reconvene the board to make the decision without considering age."

He started shaking his head. "I can't do that. You're telling me I violated the law. I can't go forward with that, and you shouldn't force me to. We made an honest and fair decision yesterday in the best interest of the organization."

"I'm not going to report this to the head of the branch, and I'm not going to report this to EEO. But I am going to tell the candidate what happened. I'll leave it to him to decide if he wants to push this."

"He won't. He's a stand-up guy and will understand why I did what I did. You do whatever you need to do."

I left his office and called the candidate. He was not as understanding as the chair had expected. And to make matters worse, Human Resources formally announced the selection of the number-one candidate that afternoon to the entire organization.

The number-two candidate made a formal EEO complaint the next morning based on my conversation with him. He also filed a lawsuit against the agency. The next few months entailed interviews and depositions from each board member, but the matter stayed unresolved for probably two years. In the end, the EEO ruling was for the candidate, and the lawsuit was settled out of court.

The chair was demoted one rank—not for his decision on the board but because he did nothing to rectify the issue when he was confronted the next day with the violation of the law. Some even argued that he had engaged in a cover-up of the incident. He was transferred to another branch and was mandated to attend numerous training "opportunities" in HR-related matters. Nothing happened to the voting members of the board, with the exception of having to attend a remedial promotion-board training course. Most important, the affected candidate was given his choice of any vacant senior manager position in the agency and received an undisclosed sum of money in damages.

I look back on that situation as one of the watershed events in my life. I was disloyal to one brother in law enforcement while exercising loyalty to another. There were plenty of other paths I could have chosen—plenty of other righteous paths. And while I believe even more today that discrimination in any form cannot be tolerated, I still do not know if I made all the best choices during that event.

## Discussion Questions

1. What other possible concerns or consequences should have been considered in this dilemma?

2. The primary decision point focused on in this chapter came after the promotion board concluded. However, Agent Gibson was required to make important decisions at several points throughout the scenario. What were some of these points?

3. How do you think you would have responded at these various decision points? How would you have responded overall to the dilemma?

# Part III

# Gifts & Gratuities

Gifts and gratuities appear in all manners and sizes—and with an equal variety of motives. Most agencies would not take exception to an officer accepting a cup of coffee from an elderly lady in her kitchen while the officer writes a larceny report. But is that any different from taking a free cup of coffee from the local convenience store? Is the motive of the giver different in these scenarios, or is the store's gesture just as harmless? Is this scenario different from accepting tickets on the fifty-yard line from a local business owner because "police officers are underpaid and are heroes in my book"?

> *We do not want our police running protection rackets; but we should be able to accept a brownie from an appreciative nun.*
> ~ Joseph Petrocelli

Motive is important in the discussion of gifts and gratuities. Yet motive is often difficult to fully grasp. One restaurant owner may offer a discount on meals out of appreciation, with no expectations. Another restaurant owner may expect special treatment—maybe letting a future speeding ticket slide or preferential attention to disturbances or crimes at his business.

As important as motive is to the discussion, it is not the only issue.

Two other implications are clear. First, the restaurant with the officer's car in the parking lot is getting more police presence and thus more crime deterrence than the restaurant down the street that does not offer police discounts. A good friend of mine's family owned a restaurant that gave free meals to police officers. Not once was that restaurant robbed or burglarized in 15 years, when nearly every other restaurant in that area was. Is this extra police presence fair and appropriate? Second, regardless of motive, what if the officer stops the restaurant owner for speeding or maybe even driving under the influence? At best, the discounted meals over time have now placed the officer in a compromising position, regardless of the restaurant owner's expectations.

The issue of gifts and gratuities is complex and stirs conflict within the police community, the scholarly world, and society. The following stories offer little to quiet this stir. What they do provide is real-life context for you, your peers, and your instructor to discuss as part of framing and developing your ethical decision-making capacity and paradigms in this area.

Although this section concludes with a classic scenario, it begins with a story that is not so typical. Yet this first situation clearly reflects two ethical issues important to gifts and gratuities: the notion that motive is not everything (this first scenario is motive-free), and the issue of officers getting something free that they would not have received without the badge.

# 9

# Where's the Harm?

*I will enforce the law courteously and appropriately without fear of favor, malice or ill will, never employing unnecessary force or violence and never accepting gratuities.*

~ International Association of Chiefs of Police

## Investigator Nick Ferguson's Story

We had been tracking a high-profile fugitive for quite some time. He was the head of a local drug organization with direct access to the Juarez cartel in Mexico. He was also responsible for ordering several deaths in the city. I got a call one evening from an informant saying he'd heard that our fugitive was staying in the Arbor Apartments on the east side of town.

I was in charge of this case, but I was kind of new to the team, so I was glad my partner was a veteran investigator with a long tenure on the squad. I gave him a call, and we were at the complex in less than an hour.

We went straight to the manager's office. She recognized the man in the photo as someone who had stayed in her complex but had been gone for at least a month. She said no one had been in that apartment for a while, the rent was three months late, and the complex had gone through the proper eviction procedures.

"If you're considering this place abandoned, do you mind if we look around inside?" I asked.

"No problem at all." She walked us to the apartment and unlocked the door, pointing to the final eviction notice hanging on it. "I've already scheduled maintenance to empty the contents of the apartment on the front lawn tomorrow morning," she said. "What the neighbors don't take, we'll take to the dump." Then she left us to our search, asking us to lock up when we left.

My partner and I went in separate directions. A few minutes later, he walked from the bedroom into the kitchen, where I was going through the drawers.

"Hey, Nick, check this out," he said. I turned to see him grinning, wearing a full-length leather duster he had apparently found in a closet. "How do I look? Nice coat, huh? It fits me perfect. And better yet, my friend, the coat is freaking abandoned property!"

You are Investigator Nick Ferguson. Reflect on these questions and considerations before reading the real-life outcome.

1. Do you give your approval (tacit or explicit) for him to take the coat?
2. Do you give your disapproval (tacit or explicit)?
3. Is there some other course of action?

## Considerations

### Position and Rank

- Both of you are the same rank.
- You are in charge of the investigation and have the authority to make decisions regarding the case.
- Your partner is senior to you in the agency and in the squad and is well respected by peers and bosses.

### Legal, Policy, and Code of Ethics Issues

- Is it legal for your partner to take the jacket? After all, it is abandoned property according to the complex manager, and it will be put in the trash tomorrow.
- Is there a policy in your agency addressing gifts and gratuities that may apply? Arguably, this is not a gift or a gratuity.
- Is there an applicable code of ethics that offers guidance in such a scenario?

### Community Impact
- If the apartment manager found out, would taking the coat have an impact on her perception of the police?
- On a neighbor's perception of the police?
- On the community's perception of the police?

## The Real-Life Decision

In that instant, I knew I was at a watershed moment in my career. Even something so small and obscure would define who I was and who I would become. I knew many others would not see the significance of the incident. But this was big to me. I had never liked the idea of a free cup of coffee, and I certainly did not like the idea of a free $500 leather coat, even if it was going to be trash tomorrow.

One of two things was no doubt occurring. Either he was asking my permission to take the coat because I was the lead investigator, or he was asking if I would keep quiet if he took it. I could have said nothing, but that would have implied my approval.

"Love the jacket. Maybe we'll all pitch in and buy you one for Christmas, cowboy," I said with a grin. "Now quit playing around and put the coat back in the closet. I need your help in here to go over these papers with me."

After a brief pause, he replied, "Give me two seconds to hang it up, and I'll be right back to help."

## Discussion Questions

1. Would taking the coat even be considered a gift or a gratuity? After all, your partner would argue that the coat is abandoned property with no giver and no motive.

2. Regardless of your answer to question 1, does this scenario present an ethical dilemma for you? Or do you believe this is such an insignificant issue that we should not even bother talking about it?

3. Do any potential negative consequences exist if he takes the coat? Where's the harm?

4. Do you agree or disagree that he would be using his badge to get something for free?

5. If you agree, does this pose a problem, or is it okay to take the coat even with that perspective?

6. Is this your call to make? Or is this a decision your partner has to make for himself?

# 10
# Plainclothes Dinner

*The impression that extra police presence can be bought for the cost of a cup of coffee or a greasy hamburger is certainly not an impression that I think the police should cultivate.*

~ Stephen Coleman

## Officer Russ Campbell's Story

There had to have been a dozen of us in the restaurant. Nearly our entire street crimes team was there for dinner, occupying the biggest table in the place. It was a small mom-and-pop restaurant, serving the best country cooking in the area—salty ham, two sides, butter biscuits, blackberry cobbler, and sweet tea. But times were tough, and the restaurant was barely making ends meet. We were the only customers there at the time. The elderly couple who owned the restaurant had no employees. He was the only cook, and she was the only waitress.

Dinner was great, and it gave our team a little downtime to get together outside work. We were usually so busy that being all in one place at the same time was rare.

The elderly woman handed the check to Paul, who was seated at the head of the table. Ever so quietly and sweetly she asked, "Sir, would you like me split the tickets, or is this one bill good for everyone? I'll be glad to do whatever is easiest for you."

"The one bill is fine, ma'am. But I think there's been a mistake with the charges," Paul said as he pointed to the final amount. He then opened his denim jacket to expose his badge, clipped on the inside pocket.

"Oh, I'm so sorry, Officer," she said. "I didn't recognize you gentlemen as the police. You sure don't look like most police officers," she said, smiling. "Let me get that discount figured in there right away."

You are Officer Russ Campbell. Reflect on these questions and considerations before reading the real-life outcome.

1. Do you say something to Paul or to the owner of the restaurant about not discounting the ticket?
2. Do you say nothing and just accept the discount?
3. Is there some other course of action?

## Considerations

### *Position and Rank*

- Paul sat at the head of the table for a reason. He is the senior guy on the squad and the informal leader of the group.
- Paul is close with the squad sergeant and lieutenant and is one of the chief's fishing and hunting buddies.

### *The Restaurant*

- The business is barely able to keep the doors open financially. They obviously cannot afford to give a police discount.
- You and your co-workers are dressed in street clothes, if that matters at all.

### *Policy, Standards of Conduct, and Code of Ethics Issues*

- Does your agency have policies or standards concerning gifts and gratuities? Does that even matter?
- Is there a police code of ethics that addresses gratuities? Does that matter?

## The Real-Life Decision

The owner walked away quickly with the check in her hand, almost like she was hurrying to avoid offending us any further. I felt horrible. I did not like the idea of accepting discounts on meals anyway. It sends the wrong message to the restaurant and the wrong message to any other patrons who may be watching. But this situation was even worse. This was not a large fast food franchise. These people absolutely could not afford to discount our food.

I remember thinking, *Is this a leadership moment I need to seize? Do I draw the line with everyone at the table?* I decided public defiance of Paul in front of everyone would be suicide. They would side with Paul anyway, and I would be ostracized from the squad. But I could not let these good people take that loss on our bill.

I patiently waited for the others to get up and throw in their few dollars of contribution. I did the same. As we all started walking out, I told them I would catch up in a couple of minutes. I had to use the restroom real quick. I went into the bathroom and waited long enough for everyone to leave. I then walked back to the kitchen, where the husband and wife were standing, and handed her $40. "Ma'am, the guys wanted you to have this."

Paul was the only one at the table that night who would have so blatantly demanded a police discount. I made it a practice from that evening forward to avoid dinners with Paul. And I somewhat rectified the problem, at least for that incident, by giving the lady enough money to cover the discount, money I really could not afford to give. But I did nothing to address the broader long-term issue.

Many years later now, I really wish I had seized that leadership moment at the table and made a stand for what was right—not to be holier than thou but simply to show the leadership that was missing that evening. I am sure I could have done it in a nonthreatening, respectful way.

Or I could have simply said, "No, Paul, we're not doing this. They can't afford to discount our meals." I think I even like that approach better. Today, I would have no problem doing that, even with more senior or higher ranked officers. I just wish I'd had that strength of character and self-confidence back then.

## Discussion Questions

1.  What is the difference between a gift and a gratuity? Is one more acceptable than the other?

2.  If you are against accepting gratuities in concept, is there a situation in which you would not take issue with their acceptance?

3.  Identify potential negative and positive consequences of accepting gifts and gratuities.

4.  A common reason for "no gratuity" policies is the *slippery slope* argument. The acceptance of even the smallest gratuity will start a predictable downward turn toward real corruption. Once an officer gets in the habit of receiving things for free, the extent of the gratuity becomes increasingly irrelevant. Even the smallest of gratuities can lead to significant corruption. What are your thoughts about the slippery slope?

# 11
# One Year From Retirement

*No one is compelled to choose the profession of
a police officer, but having chosen it, everyone is
obliged to live up to the standard of its requirements.
To join in that high enterprise means the surrender of
much individual freedom.*

~ Calvin Coolidge

## Major Jim Weaver's Story

As one of the largest police departments in the country, we certainly had our fair share of internal problems and challenges. We were also faced daily with various citizen complaints against our officers. Bias, discrimination, and prejudice seemed to account for an ever-expanding number of these complaints and subsequent lawsuits.

In an attempt to change the culture of our agency, the deputy superintendent established a working group of politicians, citizens, and academics to partner with the police to devise a plan of action. Over the next year, several new initiatives came to fruition. The one that affected me the most was the mandatory training of every officer in cultural sensitivity and tolerance.

As the commander of the police academy, it was my role to build our capacity to deliver this training to thousands of police officers over the next two years. My senior staff and I spent weeks brainstorming various strategies and questions. What would the curriculum look like? Who would build the course? How would the course be delivered (e.g., web based, face-to-face)? Who would deliver these courses? Early in our discussions, it became evident that the academy's role would be to manage the program; we did not have the time, resources, or expertise to actually build or deliver the training. We decided to look to higher education for help.

Over the next month, we engaged every university in and around our city. There were many. We narrowed our choices down to three universities (one public and two private) that had a demonstrated expertise and ability to meet all our requirements. This would be a two-year program worth millions of dollars to the winning college.

As I sat in my office one afternoon, my secretary informed me that the executive vice president of one of the two private universities was on the phone for me. I had met her once before briefly, but mostly my staff and I had been dealing with the dean of the School of Professional Education, a position two rungs down from her.

"Good afternoon, Beth. What can I do for you today?"

"Good afternoon to you, Major Weaver. Thank you for taking my call. As you probably know from our aggressive marketing campaign of recent, we are looking to extensively expand our criminal justice program. We will be looking for one or two additional professors very soon, and down the road, we'll be looking to fill senior-level management positions in these programs."

"That's very exciting. Obviously, your university has a tremendous reputation. I'm sure you'll be able to build a world-class criminal justice program."

"Major, let me ask you a personal question, if you don't mind. Have you ever thought about a career as a college professor?"

"Only for the past ten years. But it's very hard getting those positions."

"How long do you have before retirement?"

"I hope to walk out in just over a year. That will give me my maximum retirement, with thirty years on the job."

"How would you like to start teaching for us right now in an adjunct capacity? Maybe one or two classes a semester depending on what's good for you. We are willing to compensate you beyond our other part-time professors because of your rank, experience, and understanding of the training world. Then hopefully by the time you retire next year, our program will have grown to need a full-time executive position—one with your name on it."

"You should know I have only a master's degree. I don't know a single professor, even adjunct, in your school without a doctorate."

"Major, flexibility and mutual cooperation are keys to success in my world just like yours. A master's degree is fine. Can I count you in on my team?"

You are Major Jim Weaver. Reflect on these questions and considerations before reading the real-life outcome.

1. Do you accept the offer?
2. Do you reject the offer?
3. Is there another choice?

## Considerations

### *Legal and Policy Issues*

- Does your agency have relevant conflict-of-interest rules?
- Do applicable contracting laws or court cases exist?
- If this university is ultimately awarded the contract, and the other two universities discover you work there part time, your agency may sustain significant civil liability.
- Even if you do not accept the offer of employment, just the mere existence of the offer may place your agency in a legally vulnerable position, particularly if that university is awarded the contract.

### *Personal and Professional Consequences*

- Her job offer will be perceived by most as a way for her university to secure the multi-million-dollar sensitivity training contract.
- If you accept the offer, your credibility will be negatively viewed by fellow professors who possess doctorates and are making less money than you.
- Your integrity may be viewed negatively as well when they inevitably connect the training contract to your timely employment.

- What is your role in awarding the contract? Are you a decision maker? Do you make recommendations? Or do you have no influence at all? More important, what would the three universities or even the community perceive your role to be?

## The Real-Life Decision

I had one year untill retirement from the department, but that did not mean real retirement. I still had one child getting ready for college. I had always known that I would need to work for at least a few years after retiring from the force. I had been looking, but the economy was tough.

Teaching at the college level would be a great second career, and it was something I had wanted for many years. Teaching would give me a chance to give back to the youngsters coming into this field, and it was fun too. I enjoyed every minute of the many years I had taught at the police academy. And the money the university VP was offering sounded more than adequate.

But as much as I wanted that job, it seemed too good to be true. There was no way her offer came without strings, expressed or implied. Her offer was about securing the sensitivity and tolerance training contract.

I knew the right thing to do was to tell her right then that I could not accept the offer and that I would have to report our conversation to the department contracting officer. But I didn't.

"Beth, let me give this some thought. I know your offer has nothing to do with the contract negotiations, but I am still concerned with the appearance that it does. Let me get back with you tomorrow."

"Major, we want you on our team regardless of that contract. I'm hardly involved with that anyway. Just call me tomorrow. I really am excited about you coming on board."

She said all the right things, and I was a senior leader in one of the largest police agencies in the country. I had nearly thirty years on the job, with a considerable amount of training experience. Maybe she did see something unique and valuable in me.

I gave it a lot of thought that night and talked it over with my wife before going to sleep. She did not see the gray area, and she let me know that in no uncertain terms.

"Jim, get over your arrogant self. You know her offer is directly related to getting that contract. And even on the remote chance that it's not, it certainly will be seen that way by everyone involved."

"What if no one finds out? What if I don't accept the part-time job, but I do accept the full-time offer next year? What if I recuse myself from the negotiations and decision making regarding the contract but don't tell Beth? If they get the contract, she'll think I did it for her, and life is good. If they don't get the contract, well, we'll know then if the job offer was sincere."

"Jim, you're playing with fire, and honestly, you're better than this. If you're not going to listen to me, at least talk to someone at work officially. Operating in the dark on something like this will come back to bite you and our family."

First thing the next day, I called our department's legal office and explained the situation. I also called our department's contracting office. They were in lockstep agreement. I could not accept the offer, and moreover, they were going to consider dropping the university from the final list of three for impropriety.

Legal also congratulated me for doing the right thing. "Major, I don't know how many executives in your position would have come forward on something like this. And you know if you had not, and we eventually found out, we would have come after you civilly and potentially criminally. You're a good man, sir."

I laughed to myself, thinking, *Yeah, a good man with a great woman at home keeping me on the straight and narrow path.*

## Discussion Questions

1. Does this conflict-of-interest story fit appropriately within a section titled "Gifts & Gratuities"? Support your position.

2. Should ethical behavior in the public service field be driven by perceptions, as conflict-of-interest policies may be, or only by reality? Explain.

3. What do you think about the real-life decision? Imagining yourself outside the classroom, dealing with this in real life, what do you think you would have done?

# Part IV

# Use of Force

The use of force by law enforcement has extensive social and legal consequences and is thus an important topic in the ethics field. Effective policing requires the appropriate use of force to fulfill its enforcement, prevention, and protection responsibilities. When the amount of force is perceived as excessive or unnecessary, however, societal approval of the broader law enforcement community is weakened.

Considerable thought was given as to which scenarios should be included in this section—there certainly were many. In keeping with one of the main themes of the book, I did not want to offer situations so egregious that the correct answers were obvious. With this in mind, I decided on the first two stories because, although not sensational or newsworthy,

> *The police must be prepared to use force under circumstances in which its rationale is often morally, legally, and practically ambiguous.*
> ~Jennifer Hunt

they represent the daily challenges officers face in this arena. The third story in this section, however, did make headlines. It is this story that truly forces an inward examination of your values and notions about right and wrong at their deepest levels.

# 12
# One Extra Hit

*While recognizing the need to demonstrate
authority and control over criminal suspects and
prisoners, officers shall adhere to this agency's
use-of-force policy and shall observe the civil rights
and protect the well-being of those in their charge.*
~ IACP Model Policy on Standards of Conduct

## Officer Maurice Banks's Story

I generally avoided running radar in the early evening because of dense traffic congestion, but traffic was unusually light today. I pulled over in a commercial parking lot facing north in the 35-mph zone of Route 30. I went through the routine calibration checks on the radar and then pulled out my paperwork for court the next day. This would be a good time for a little case preparation.

Within a couple of minutes, I heard a high pitch on the radar and then *85 mph* beeped across the screen as a green crotch rocket flew by me. I pulled out quickly and hit the lights and siren. Over the past few months, the south side had experienced a rash of motorcycle thefts from dealerships and private residences. Maybe this was more than a speeding violation.

The Kawasaki Ninja accelerated to the next intersection and turned on Route 3, heading toward the city. I called in the pursuit to Dispatch and instantly heard sirens coming my way from several directions. In less than a minute, we were crossing the jurisdiction line.

Several city officers immediately picked up the pursuit while I started dropping back, but I stayed close enough to maintain a visual on the bike. The motorcycle took a sudden turn into an apartment complex that I knew had only one way in and out because of construction. As I entered the complex behind the city officers, I saw the motorcycle crash and the rider take off running. Several city officers started chasing on foot. I jumped out of my car and tried to catch up, but I lost them for a minute as they turned a corner, out of sight. When I rounded the building, I saw the handcuffed rider face down on the ground. One of the city cops then rolled him over and drove his fist hard right into the rider's mouth.

As I approached, I heard the officer quietly but firmly utter in the rider's ear, "Don't you *ever* run from the law again!"

You are Officer Maurice Banks. Reflect on these questions and considerations before reading the real-life outcome.

1.  Do you report the city police officer for improper use of force?
2.  Do you ignore what happened?
3.  Is there some other course of action?

## Considerations

### Personal and Professional Consequences

*   If this one hit gets out to the public, and you have not reported it, what will happen to you?
*   If you let this slide just one time, will you be trapped by that decision forever?
*   What happens to you if you turn in another officer?

### Community Impact

*   What if a private citizen saw what you saw? Or worse, what if it was videotaped?
*   Could an incident like this spark not only subtle tension between the police and the community, but an actual civil outpouring against the entire department, particularly if none of the officers present did anything to stop the act or report it after it occurred?
*   What if this hit actually drove home the point so clearly with the motorcycle driver that he never runs from the police again, thus potentially saving his life and the lives of other officers and citizens?

## The Real-Life Decision

I walked over and helped the prisoner to his feet. I switched out the handcuffs that were on him with my handcuffs. As I started walking him back to my car, I turned and looked each officer in the eye, saying with contempt, "Thanks, guys, for helping out this afternoon. I hope you had fun."

Once in the car, I saw no visible marks on the guy's face, and he offered no complaints. The hit was never brought up again.

I wonder today, many years later and many ranks higher, if I had been too weak that day, or if my lack of action was appropriate. I don't know how many more punches it would have taken for me to report that city cop. Maybe just one more would have tipped the scale. I wasn't even sure at the time that the hit did not serve some greater purpose, maybe preventing him from running from the police in the future. Plus, there was the small sense of street justice and the deep solidarity that all police officers share. This job is often harder than it looks.

## Discussion Questions

1. Assuming most agencies have a reporting requirement of their officers for such incidents, would that policy affect your decision here?

2. Identify potential unintended consequences of reporting and not reporting this incident. Think in terms of self, other officers, the agency, and the community.

3. Assume the hit was reported by a bystander, and you had not reported the incident, just as the county officer did not in the real-life scenario. You are called to testify about your observations. Do you now admit what you saw, risking administrative sanctions against yourself as well as social stigma among your peers? Or do you lie, thus triggering lying-under-oath implications?

4. Do you believe that the hit, while the rider was handcuffed, could serve a greater purpose? If so, do the means justify the end?

5. Does this scenario even represent a dilemma for you? If not, is it clear to you that you would report or would not report the city officer?

# 13
# Loosen Those Cuffs

*That old law about 'an eye for an eye' leaves everybody blind. The time is always right to do the right thing.*

~ Martin Luther King, Jr.

## Officer Bryan Burke's Story

We sometimes view use of force in the context of high-profile incidents, such as Rodney King in Los Angeles or Abner Louima in New York. But the police use force, or the threat of force, in a variety of much smaller ways every day. And beyond any doubt, this force is rarely abused.

My story is not glamorous. It does not involve a group of cops beating someone or shooting a fleeing felon. I'm not even sure the type of force in my story can be found on a Use of Force Continuum. This story, rather, is about the type of force issue that officers confront much more frequently.

Highway patrol (HP) officers work alone. The HP also works on a separate radio system than local police departments. It's a dangerous job, so local officers like me try to help whenever possible.

I had just finished processing a drunk driver I'd arrested earlier in the evening. It was a busy Friday night, so I needed to get back in service and back to my beat. I jumped on the interstate and headed north. About two miles down the highway, I came upon an HP officer who had a van pulled over. It was just him and several males on the side of the highway. I marked out and pulled over behind his cruiser.

Before I could even get to the van, things went south fast. Two of the men took off running, and two jumped the HP officer. Between cap stun and a couple swings of the baton, we were able to get the situation under control. While both prisoners were secured by local officers who had just arrived, the HP officer and I searched the van. We found five pounds of marijuana. And the GPS had the active location they were going to with the drugs. With the HP officer's concurrence, he would take both arrests, but any subsequent drug investigation would be handled by my department.

The HP officer secured the marijuana, and the other two local officers agreed to impound the van and search it more thoroughly. I put one prisoner in my patrol car, and the HP officer put the other in his car. We then headed to the county magistrate's office, which was adjacent to the jail.

We started down the sidewalk together, with his prisoners in tow. The HP officer's prisoner was really complaining about the handcuffs, but his complaints were being completely ignored.    Right before we got to the door to the building, I asked the HP officer to stop a minute while I looked at his prisoner's wrists, which were starting to bleed.

"Brother, these cuffs are on way too tight. You need to loosen them before we go inside."

"Screw him." Then looking at the prisoner, he remarked, "Maybe you'll think twice about jumping a cop next time."

I understood his anger, but this wasn't the way to cope with it. "Look, I feel you, but his wrists are bleeding. This isn't cool. Loosen those cuffs."

"These are my prisoners. Now open the door."

I opened the door and released one handcuff on my prisoner, securing it to the steel bench in the waiting area. The HP officer took his time with his prisoner. I could see his wrists getting worse from several feet away.

The deputy sheriff running intake came out to watch the prisoners while the HP officer and I went back to explain the events on the interstate to the magistrate. It took about twenty minutes for the magistrate to type the arrest warrants.

When we returned, the deputy had a physical injury report out. Looking at the HP officer, he said, "This guy's wrists are in bad shape. What happened?"

The HP officer responded, "I checked them twice before putting him in my car. They were fine. They were loose, if anything. Then we noticed just a few minutes ago that he had tightened them and caused all this bruising and bleeding by squirming in them. He did all that to himself."

Then the deputy looked at me. "Is that correct, Officer?"

You are Officer Bryan Burke. Reflect on these questions and considerations before reading the real-life outcome.

1. Do you corroborate the HP officer's story?
2. Do you tell the truth about what happened and the conversation you had with the HP officer before entering the building?
3. Is there some other course of action?

## Considerations

### *The Blue Wall of Silence*
- Cops protect one another . . .
- But only to a point.
- Relations with the state highway patrol will be affected by this decision. Protecting the HP officer will strengthen this bond. Standing against him may even start turf battles, with the agencies entering a ticketing war against each other and refusing to back one another on calls.

### *The Role of the Police*
- Who is better positioned to protect the police than the police?
- Who is better positioned to impart justice immediately?
- Our government is designed with checks and balances. The police arrest and serve as witness to events and aspects of the investigation. The courts adjudicate and dispense any punitive recourse.

## The Real-Life Decision

"I saw his left wrist starting to bleed before we came inside. I don't know anything beyond that."

In an instant, I had made a decision that blood is thicker than water. I just kept thinking, *Cops don't dime out other cops.* No, I did not throw my full support behind the HP officer, but I clearly gave my tacit support by playing ignorant. Without my full disclosure of the handcuffs being too tight and the conversation outside demonstrating the HP officer's desire for vengeance, this incident was not going anywhere.

Those two dirt bags deserved a lot more than they got in the justice system months later. They had jumped a police officer on the side of the highway. What would they have done to the officer if I had not stopped that evening? Maybe the temporary pain in that guy's wrist would cause him to pause next time he thought about fighting a cop.

So, personally, I couldn't care less about a bruised and bloody wrist. But that doesn't mean I believe it is the role of the police to impose retribution, even on a smaller scale like this. That's up to the courts, whether they do a good job of it or not.

That incident was seventeen years ago, and I still remember it like it was yesterday. I've seen much worse over the years, but that one stuck with me for some reason . . . maybe because I had the chance to be a leader before even walking in the building that night.

## Discussion Questions

1. The primary decision point in this scenario was framed at the moment when the deputy sheriff asked the local officer, "Is that correct?" Were there other important decision points prior to or potentially after this one? Explain.

2. Do you agree or disagree with the real-life decision? Should Officer Burke have done more? Less? Or was his behavior appropriate? Explain.

3. Regardless of whether you agree or disagree with the real-life decision, do you believe that the retributive justice applied by the HP officer could serve a greater purpose in protecting future police officers? Or could the incident incite vengeance in the heart of the prisoner, causing undue harm to officers in the future?

# 14
# Dark Justice

*Justice is the firm and continuous desire to render to everyone that which is his due.*

~Justinian I

## Game Warden Terrance Larson's Story

"Dispatch, GW 130. I need backup! . . . shots . . ."

"GW 130, repeat your traffic. . . . GW 130, status." There was no response to Dispatch.

Fresh out of college three years ago, Travis had found the perfect career, a place where his love of the outdoors and his passion for public service intertwined. Yet, Travis joining the Bureau of Game and Inland Fisheries may have meant more to me than to him. I had been a game warden for over twenty years in the same district. Now my son-in-law was following in my steps. Travis had married my only child, Vanessa, one week after they'd graduated from college. Two years later, I was a grandfather of the most beautiful girl, and now another grandchild was on the way.

"GW 36 en route," I responded. Unless a state trooper or sheriff's deputy happened to be out that way, I was the closest backup, and I was eight miles away. "GW 36 to GW 130. . . . GW 36 to GW 130. . . . Travis, talk to me, son!" I had never experienced a more terrifying silence in my life.

Travis had gone to serve a summons on a guy for illegal trapping. This was a fairly minor offense. Travis would have had the man simply sign a summons promising to appear in court.

"GW 36 to Dispatch, three minutes out."

"10-4, GW 36. Closest backup unit ETA . . . eight minutes."

"10-4. Any information on the resident of the house?"

"Roger, GW 36. Owner of residence has extensive criminal record—multiple violent crimes.

"GW 36, on scene."

I came in hot on the gravel driveway. Travis's SUV was there, with no Travis in sight. Twenty feet away was a white male standing at another car with the trunk open.

I drew down on him. "Police, hands in the air!"

It happened so fast and furious. He turned and started coming directly at me, with a wave of bullets pummeling my vehicle. I was being engaged with automatic fire. The second the rapid fire paused, I stood up without thinking and emptied my pistol in his direction. He had closed the distance to about ten feet. He went down.

I changed magazines in my pistol and ran toward him. He was covered in blood. It was hard to see exactly where I'd hit him, but it looked like maybe in the leg and shoulder. I flipped him over and cuffed his wrists behind his back. From the ensuing scream, it was pretty clear his shoulder had taken a shot.

"GW 36, Dispatch."

"Go GW 36."

"Gunfight with one male. He's down. I don't see GW 130 yet. Where's backup? There may be more armed suspects in the house."

"Multiple officers en route; three minutes ETA."

"10-4."

All I could think was that my son might be in that house, and he didn't have three minutes. I had to hit the house hard and fast. Maybe the surprise would give me some fighting chance if it was an ambush.

I ran toward the car with the open trunk to give me a little cover before assaulting the house. My God . . . there was a rolled-up rug covered in blood in the trunk. *Lord, please don't be Travis.* I cut the rope from around the rug. It was Travis, the son I had been blessed with three years ago, the father of my granddaughter, and the husband of my expecting daughter. There was no pulse, no life in him to save.

I slowly walked back toward the bloody prisoner handcuffed on the ground. I rolled him over and looked directly in his eyes. "Did you kill that officer?"

Spitting up blood, he looked at me with contempt. "You damn right I did."

This man didn't deserve to live. He had killed my son, a twenty-six-year-old police officer, and would kill again one day. He needed to die right then and there. I could hear sirens closing in the distance.

You are Game Warden Terrance Larson (GW 36). Reflect on these questions and considerations before reading the real-life outcome.

1. Do you exact what you believe to be justice and execute the man?
2. Do you wait for backup and allow the criminal justice system to dispense justice?
3. Is there some other course of action?

## Considerations

### *Legal Issues*

- The suspect was handcuffed and posed no imminent threat at the decision point. Shooting the suspect would be a homicide. If caught, your actions might also be considered premeditated (possessing malice aforethought), thus triggering capital murder implications.
- If caught, you may have potential defenses to mitigate a murder conviction (e.g., insanity, provocation, heat of passion).

### *Moral Issues*

- The suspect has a history of violence and may kill again.
- The suspect just killed a police officer, a young man in the prime of his life.
- What if the criminal justice system does not work—he gets off on a technicality, for example. Or he waits on death row for the rest of his life. Is this justice?

- Why should he live when your son-in-law will not?
- Why should he live when your grandchildren will never have a father?
- Killing him will not bring back your loss.
- Killing him may cause additional loss to your family if you are imprisoned for murder.
- Killing him in cold blood goes against everything you have ever learned or stood for in the service to your community and society.

## The Real-Life Decision

I stood him up, took two steps back to avoid the clear signs of an execution-style murder, and then put two bullets in his chest. I rolled him back over on his side with my foot and went back to Travis.

As ambulances, sheriff's deputies, and state troopers arrived, I just sat in the driveway holding Travis's body. An officer, a member of my family, was dead. The adrenaline started wearing off, and the pain of the loss started to ache.

I also began having physical pain. Unknown to me, I had been shot in my side. A helicopter landed in a field just down the road, and I was taken to the nearest hospital and admitted. The bullet missed any major organs, but I had lost a significant amount of blood.

The next day, the director of Game and Inland Fisheries and the state police administrator visited me at the hospital. "Terry, we're very sorry for your family's loss. Travis was a good man."

"Thank you, sir. He sure was."

"We're hearing you're going to be fine physically, but you'll have to give the emotional wounds some time. We're all here for as long as it takes to get back on your feet."

"I'll be fine. I am worried about my famil, but we'll get through this. Sir, I heard while I was on the stretcher that no one else was in the house?"

"That's right. But we did find an arsenal of automatic and high-powered weapons and ammunition."

"Have the crime scene guys reconstructed the scene yet to see what exactly happened to Travis?"

"They're telling us that Travis was ambushed at the front door . . . shot over forty times . . . never had time to even draw his pistol. And for what it's worth, Terry, the forensics guys are telling us that you're a hero. All the evidence indicates a 100 percent good shoot on your part."

"Sir, there's something we need to talk about."

## Discussion Questions

1.  What other consequences and implications should Game Warden Larson have considered before making his decision?

2.  Game Warden Larson took an oath over twenty years ago to uphold the Constitution and the laws of his state and country. Does he have a greater responsibility to the service of justice that may override this oath? Does he have a right at all to determine what justice is in this situation?

3.  Does this story even present a quandary for you? If not, which choice is so clear for you that no dilemma exists? Explain.

# Part V

## Search & Seizure

Society has granted police officers significant power in the quest to protect and serve. Officers have the authority to deprive persons of their liberty. Indeed, they have the power to take someone's life under certain conditions. Officers also have the authority to search citizens and their most private belongings and to seize evidence, contraband, and proceeds from illegal activities. While policies and laws define the powers and limitations of the police in this area, the Fourth Amendment to the United States Constitution is the core of search and seizure law.

The Fourth Amendment is fundamentally about privacy from unreasonable government intrusion. We want our law enforcement officers to have the ability to protect us from evil doers, yet we are passionately sensitive as a society to ensure the government does not overstep the powers afforded it.

> *One of the most essential branches of English liberty is the freedom of one's house. A man's house is his castle; and while his is quiet, he is well guarded as a prince in his castle.*
> ~ James Otis

Most police officers keenly understand their powers, authorities, and limitations with regard to search and seizure. Most try to abide by these governing laws and rules each and every day. Yet abuses do happen—most inadvertent, some intentional. The courts have taken an aggressive position against unreasonable searches and seizures. The two most significant judicial outcomes have been the Exclusionary Rule and the Fruits of the Poisonous Tree Doctrine.

The Exclusionary Rule holds that evidence seized as the result of an illegal search cannot be used as direct evidence against the defendant in a criminal proceeding. The Fruits of the Poisonous Tree Doctrine takes this position further. In addition to evidence from an unreasonable search being excluded, that evidence may not be used to discover other evidence. Together, these rules attempt to ensure that both the tree and any potential fruit from that tree are inadmissible in court.

With the voluminous amount of policies, statutes, laws, court cases, and even our Constitution placing such significance on this area, it would seem that search and seizure issues would not provide significant ethical difficulties. Yet, as you will observe in the following stories, the search and seizure arena offers some of the most challenging ethical dilemmas in law enforcement.

# 15
# Four Twenty-Dollar Rocks

*Ethics is what you do in the dark when*
*no one's watching.*
~Rushworth Kidder

## Officer Craig Hopkins's Story

Nate and I were the only two "jump out" officers working that Saturday night. Our job usually consisted of buying drugs from a street corner, with the rest of our team "jumping out" of the van to make the arrest. I think it was the immediate gratification of our work that made it so rewarding.

We didn't usually do jump outs with just two officers, but we knew we could handle the one guy standing close to the back of that section 8 complex.

"You holding?" Nate asked.

"Yeah, what you need?" asked the dealer.

"You got twenties?" I asked. "We want four."

He handed me four $20 rocks of crack in exchange for eight $10 bills. I slammed opened my car door while shoving the little Ziploc baggies in my pocket. Nate exited the car quickly as well to make the arrest. We had a little foot pursuit, but nothing too long and not much of a resistance. We had him in the car and headed to processing before his crowd had time to react.

After we finished the booking process, we field tested the cocaine in our office and packaged it to go to the state lab for official testing. I stored it in our overnight drug room. The next day, I signed the cocaine into the official evidence room. Several days later, I signed out those drugs as well as drugs from three other cases. Nate and I took all of it to the state lab, which was an hour away.

About a month later, I was over in the city on another matter and decided to stop by the lab to pick up whatever evidence was ready. I signed out several packages and took them straight to our evidence room.

Another month passed, and now it was time for court regarding the four $20 rocks. About an hour before court, I stopped by evidence control to sign out the drugs.

"Craig, those drugs are still at the lab. We have you signing that package out to take to the lab but never signing it back in," the property clerk said.

This was crazy. Court was in an hour, and I had forgotten to get the drugs. Maybe at least I could get the lab to fax over the official report, assuming it was complete. I called a friend at the lab.

"Hey, I'm in a pinch here. Can you check to see if this case is finished?" I gave him the evidence numbers and the date I'd submitted the drugs.

"My friend, you picked up these drugs a month ago along with three other cases. I'm looking at the paperwork right now that you signed."

I immediately had the property control clerk check her records for that day. "Yes, I see you turning back in several cases from the lab on that date. One, two, three . . . looks like you turned in three cases," she explained.

"That's not possible," I said, with probably a little anxiety in my voice. "There has to be four cases."

"I will go through every nook and cranny this morning, but it is what it is. You never turned them back in to evidence control."

I went to court and explained to the district attorney that I apparently had not picked up the drugs from the state lab yet, but I did have a faxed copy of the official drug report. He was expecting a guilty plea but would still need the drugs to offer as evidence. He postponed the case another thirty days.

I spent those thirty days searching every car in the squad, every parking lot, my house, trash cans . . . everywhere I could think of. The plastic baggie containing the four rocks were gone. This was a serious situation. Losing evidence not only meant the dealer would go free, but it could also lead to a public relations disaster, showcasing the police department's incompetence. And it certainly meant I would be charged internally with losing evidence—a career ender in my agency. One month had passed, and I had told no one. Court was just a couple of days away.

"Nate, we need to talk." I explained what had happened.

"Well, there is a very simple solution to all of this. It is illegal but not immoral," Nate suggested.

"There's no such thing."

"You know that whole drawer in the office full of those rocks of soap that we used to sell to people as crack when we were doing those stings?"

"Yeah, so?" I wasn't following him at this point.

"Look, take four of those soap rocks out and package them just as those original four rocks had been packaged. Tell evidence control you found the drugs. Then sign them in for two days, sign them back out for court, and then turn them over in court for destruction. The rocks will be destroyed in less than two weeks. Dilemma over—"

"Nate, are you out of your mind? I would have to turn them in at court under oath. I'd be committing perjury!"

"Yeah, I said it would be illegal. But look, the cocaine that guy sold us really was cocaine. You have the official lab report documenting that. It's not like you're planting evidence. There's nothing morally wrong with doing this. In fact, it's more wrong to let him go free when he's getting ready to plead guilty to cocaine distribution. It's just no big deal, and no one will ever know. Do it and move on."

You are Officer Craig Hopkins. Reflect on these questions and considerations before reading the real-life outcome.

1. Do you submit the fake crack as evidence?
2. Do you dismiss Nate's suggestion and go to your sergeant about the matter?
3. Is there some other course of action?

## Considerations

### Legal Issues

- Following Nate's suggestion would be against the law. The legal consequences would be severe if you were caught.
- If you make any attempt to follow Nate's suggestion, it may be considered felony conspiracy as well. Both you and Nate would face criminal charges.

### Professional Consequences

- You are next on the promotion list to make sergeant. Clearly, that will not happen if you report this incident through your chain of command. Losing evidence could, in effect, end your career.
- If you go through with Nate's plan and get caught, you will unequivocally be fired. Your days as a law enforcement officer anywhere will be over for good.

### Moral Issues

- The defendant will go free if you tell the truth.
- You will have to live with whatever decision you make for the rest of your life.

## The Real-Life Decision

For a few seconds, I actually thought through what Nate was suggesting. I know my response should have been clear and immediate, but he had some good points. And I was fearful for my career, which was climbing fast. Yet I had never done anything remotely like this. I had lived my career playing by the rules and doing what I thought was morally right.

"No, Nate, I can't do it. Besides the fear of getting caught, I just can't lie in court. That's something that once you do, there's no going back."

"I understand completely," Nate said. "It was just a suggestion. I'm in your corner no matter what happens from here on out."

I first called the assistant district attorney and explained everything. He was great. "No worries, Officer. This is a real shame, and I know you're going to get hit pretty hard in your department for this. But the defendant is looking at eight years of comeback time on a previous distribution charge. He'll still be going to prison even though this actual offense will have to be dropped."

I explained everything to my sergeant that evening. He was furious—not so much about the lost drugs as about how long I had waited to report it. I'll never forget the chastising he gave me.

"You just made every one of us look like crap. The entire jump out team now looks like liars who try to avoid the truth!"

"I know, Sergeant. . . . I feel awful about this. I really stepped in it this time."

"Look, you're an honest guy and a great cop. Let's go together right now to IA [Internal Affairs]. I'll be with you every step of the way. Okay?"

With that, we walked to the building next door and met with the IA lieutenant personally. For the next eight months, IA shredded the jump out team, going through years of cases and every move we had ever made. They interviewed (interrogated) each of us—some of us more than once. They had questions that never came to my mind. Did I "lose" the drugs on purpose because the defendant paid me off? Was my sergeant or lieutenant culpable because of poor oversight or weak procedures and processes? Were we all loose cannons who did not take our duties seriously?

When it was all over, I took a hit but not as bad as it could have been. The IA lieutenant summoned me to the chief's office. They explained the entire investigation and the results. I was found guilty of the internal charge of neglect of duty (for loss/mishandling of evidence that resulted in the dismissal of a felony indictment). I received one day of suspension for the neglect of duty and five days for not reporting the incident sooner.

"I want to tell you something more important than everything else," the chief continued. "The lieutenant tells me that eight months of investigation into your team has left him completely convinced that you are one of the most ethical officers in this department. Lesser men would have responded in, well, let's say, lesser ways. You still have a bright future with this department."

## Discussion Questions

1. Do you agree with the real-life decision or would you have decided differently? Explain.

2. Setting aside the consequences of potentially getting caught, do you think Officer Hopkins still made the right choice?

3. If you agree that Officer Hopkins should report the lost evidence, should he have reported the incident at the actual time he knew the drugs were lost, which was a month earlier, or was it appropriate to take the extra time hoping the drugs would be found?

# 16
# K-9 Probable Cause

*Whoever is careless with the truth in small matters*
*cannot be trusted with important matters.*

~Albert Einstein

## Trooper Daniel Holt's Story

Traffic stops are probably the most common occasion for police officers to use drug dogs. The courts have consistently ruled that using a trained and certified dog and handler to sniff the exterior of a lawfully stopped vehicle is not considered a search under the Fourth Amendment. The underlying premise to these rulings is that no reasonable expectation of privacy exists in the air around a vehicle. Of course, "running the dog" on a vehicle must be done expeditiously within a reasonable time after stopping the vehicle. What determines reasonableness will depend on the specific circumstances surrounding the stop. Even with limitations, canines are a powerful tool in the fight against illegal drugs.

My state police agency received a Crime Stoppers tip that a 1999 Chevrolet Silverado pickup truck with Georgia license plates, blue exterior, and gray cloth interior, would be passing through my district in about thirty minutes on Interstate 95. The bed of the truck would have a heavy duty cover over it. Inside the bed would be 2,000 pounds of marijuana extensively wrapped in various packaging with layers of strongly scented materials to mask the smell.

This was all the information I had. Even if I saw the truck, I did not have sufficient probable cause to search it. My plan was simple. My partner and I would wait in two different areas of Interstate 95. If we spotted the vehicle, we would follow it in hopes of developing reasonable suspicion to pull it over. This part was fairly easy. The truck would probably have some defect, or the driver would commit a minor traffic offense, like not signaling when making a lane change. Searching the vehicle after the stop would be the hard part.

Consent to search would be my first option, but I needed a backup plan if that didn't work. As soon as I left the district station, heading toward the interstate, I called the local police department for assistance from their K-9 unit. The dog's estimated time of arrival was thirty minutes.

My partner spotted the truck at 7:52 p.m. "Bravo 1401 to 1512."

"Go for 1512," I responded.

"Target vehicle spotted northbound at exit 248. I'm pulling out on him now. Looks like one white male driving with no visible passengers."

"Roger that—three minutes out."

As I caught up to my partner, he radioed, "1512, I don't know if you can see from your position, but his left rear taillight is completely out. Are you ready to make the stop?"

"10-4. Do it. I'll see how close the K-9 unit is."

The truck was just as the Crime Stoppers tip had described. But as anticipated, my partner and I could not smell marijuana coming from it, and we could not see under the bed cover. We asked the driver for consent to search the truck, but he refused, saying he didn't have time.

The police K-9 officer arrived within five minutes of our stop and had witnessed most of the conversation with the driver. The officer said,

"Well, looks like I'm on. Sound good, Trooper?"

"Absolutely, and hey, thanks for coming up here and helping us out tonight."

The officer retrieved his dog from his police SUV and started walking toward the blue truck. Then he stopped and walked back to me. With his voice lowered, he said, "So, Trooper, I don't know what you're looking for exactly, or what PC [probable cause] you have or don't have, but if you want my dog to hit, he'll hit." With a wink and a grin, he continued, "Just say the word, boss."

You are Trooper Daniel Holt. Reflect on these questions and considerations before reading the real-life outcome.

1. Do you accept the K-9 officer's offer?
2. Do you turn it down?
3. Is there another course of action?

## Considerations

### *Legal, Personal, and Professional Consequences*

- You may not have a legal way to search the truck. Thus, not searching may allow a potentially guilty man to go free, along with $2 million in marijuana.
- Searching the vehicle in this circumstance without probable cause is an illegal search with significant implications. Should you be caught:
  - ° Any evidence found in the truck will almost certainly be suppressed, letting a guilty man go free.
  - ° You and your agency will be exposed to substantial civil liability.
  - ° If you keep your job, any testimony for the rest of your career will be tainted, in effect making you irrelevant to the state police.
  - ° In many states, conducting an illegal search has legally specified consequences, such as termination from employment and never being able to serve as a police officer again.

### *The K-9 Officer*

- With his offer to you, he has shown a willingness to:
  - ○ Break the law.
  - ○ Violate constitutional protections afforded every citizen.
  - ○ Place significant civil liability and risk on his department and yours.
  - ○ Violate the trust the community has given him.

## The Real-Life Decision

"No, my friend, don't do me any favors. If your dog hits, that's fine. If he doesn't hit, that's fine too."

"Sounds good. Wish me luck." The officer shrugged as he and his dog turned toward the truck.

The dog did alert on the truck. It was one of the strongest alerts I had ever seen. We secured the driver and uncovered the truck bed. Just as the Crime Stoppers tip had indicated, the entire rear of the truck was packed with marijuana. The level of sophistication with the packaging was remarkable and exceeded anything I had ever seen.

This was the largest drug seizure of my career. And the arrests and seizures kept flowing over the next year as the feds got involved and threw their resources and international connections into the investigation.

Not once did I ever doubt the veracity of the dog alert that evening. I had seen hundreds of alerts and nonalerts over the years. This was as clear a hit as it gets. But I still wonder if I should have done more than just turn that K-9 officer's offer down. My guess is that his offer to me would have been enough to have the evidence suppressed. So you could say I intentionally withheld exculpatory evidence from the defense. That is serious business and grinds at me even today, many years later. Of course, letting a clearly guilty man (and all the subsequent other drug dealers who were arrested and convicted) go free would not have sat well with me either.

And then there's the issue of the unscrupulous K-9 officer. By my silence, he continued in his position for many years. Who knows how many fake alerts occurred on his watch? Who knows how many law-abiding citizens were harassed and searched because of him? In fact, if that officer was willing to lie in this situation, and subsequently perjure himself when the case went to trial, maybe he has lied under oath in countless other investigations. Maybe his K-9 and drug units are entirely corrupt. I mean, who knows?

Making ethical choices in our world is extremely difficult. It's easy to say "do the right thing," but figuring out what the right thing is, at every step, is sometimes overwhelming. Whether to accept the K-9 officer's offer on I-95 was only the first ethical decision I had to make. I did well there. But did I do as well over the following days, weeks, and months?

## Discussion Questions

1. The truck fit the description of the Crime Stoppers tip exactly. The time the truck came through was spot on. Every morsel of Trooper Holt's experience told him marijuana was in the truck's bed. Yet probable cause was just not quite there. Do you agree with his declination of the K-9 officer's offer, or should he have maybe winked back and said, "Do what you think is right, my friend. Any help I can get is always appreciated."

2. In the real-life decision, Trooper Holt did not compromise his integrity or ask the K-9 officer to compromise his. But clearly, the K-9 officer's sense of right and wrong was compromised before he arrived at the traffic stop. Was Trooper Holt correct to simply say no to the officer and leave it at that? Or should Trooper Holt have reported the officer's behavior? Reporting the officer would have effectively ruined his career and potentially nullified years of convictions previous to that night—convictions of truly guilty drug dealers. Not reporting the officer may have meant jeopardizing the rights of countless citizens for years.

# 17

# One Black Hair

*I recognize the badge of my office as a symbol of public faith, and I accept it as a public trust to be held so long as I am true to the ethics of the police service. I will constantly strive to achieve these objectives and ideals, dedicating myself before God to my chosen profession . . . law enforcement.*

~ IACP Code of Ethics

## Officer Timothy Vaughn's Story

"Delta 40, with unit to back, copy a call: E Street Apartments, elderly female assaulted in home, bound and gagged. Rescue in route. Attempting to obtain more information."

"Copy. Delta 40 en route," I responded. Several other officers also responded that they were en route to either the residence or to the area to be on the lookout for the suspect once a description was given.

We still did not have much information from Dispatch. We were updated before arrival that the elderly woman's children had found her severely beaten, bound, and unconscious. The family said that no one else was in the apartment to their knowledge.

I was the third officer on the scene. As I approached the front door, I saw Officer John Fearing trying to calm the family. "The apartment is secure," he said. "No one else is here. Bret is with the victim in the

back bedroom. We need the apartment and surrounding area secured…
10-79." A 10-79 meant the victim was dead. This entire area was now
a murder scene.

I went down the hall to the bedroom to see if Bret wanted Rescue to
come in to make the declaration or if would he do it. He replied, "Tim,
stand here at the door for me. I'll get a paramedic to come in."

I had been out of the academy for one year, and this was my first
murder scene. The woman was lying on the floor several feet into the
room. For some reason, maybe just curiosity, I walked in the bedroom
and stood overlooking her body for a few seconds, then walked back to
the door. Bret approached shortly afterward with one paramedic in tow
to make the official pronouncement.

"Hey, Tim. No one has been in this room while I was gone, right?"

"That's right. No one's been in there."

The rest of the morning was like any murder scene. Forensics scoured
the apartment. The medical examiner was at the scene. Officers and detectives went door-to-door looking for leads. The MO here followed a
similar pattern of elderly rapes over the past three months. This, however, was the first homicide.

Two weeks later at roll call, the sergeant started with some news
about the murder. "You know about the serial rapist situation in the
community. The murder two weeks ago in the E Street Apartments,
which we believe was committed by this same rapist, has hit an obsta-
cle. Forensics has accounted for every hair found in that bedroom but
two—one black strand from a white male, and one black strand from
a black male. From the FBI profile and evidence at the various scenes,
detectives believe the suspect is a black male. But what if they're wrong
and chasing the wrong person? What if we have a copy cat now? I need
you to double your efforts on the street. Shake every informant. Get
every lead you can."

Having two Italian parents, I had the thickest, blackest hair of anyone at roll call that morning. And I had been in that bedroom, if only for a few seconds. What if the black hair from the white male was mine? I needed to talk to the detectives, but I had told Bret at the crime scene that I had not been in the room, that no one had. And I had made matters worse by not signing the bedroom ledger acknowledging that I had been in that room.

I had known right from the beginning that entering the room was a mistake. At the time, I hadn't wanted to make matters worse by calling attention to it. So I had lied to Bret *and* hadn't signed the ledger that day. This was big. My hands and forehead began to sweat as my stomach wrenched in knots.

You are Officer Timothy Vaughn. Reflect on these questions and considerations before reading the real-life outcome.

1. Do you come forward and admit that you were in the bedroom that day?
2. Do you remain quiet and hope that the case gets solved with your career still intact?

## Considerations

### *Professional Consequences*

• If you had not lied to Bret and had signed the ledger, you would have been ridiculed for making a rookie mistake, but nothing more. Instead, you lied orally and, indirectly, in writing. Coming forward at this point will have career consequences.

### *Moral Issues*

• If Forensics cannot match the hair strands, detectives will spend extremely valuable time and resources conducting, in effect, two investigations. Indeed, the entire investigation could be thrown off the true killer if they start down a false path.
• If a suspect is arrested as a result of one of those hair strands, the defense will make a strong argument that the other, unidentified person was the killer.
• Maybe, even probably, it was not your hair anyway. Yet is that a chance you are willing to take?

## The Real-Life Decision

I left roll call and drove to my beat. I wrote two traffic tickets, responded to a commercial vandalism and a residential larceny, both from the night before, and stopped by a few stores in the spirit of community policing. But the entire morning, I was consumed with the decision I had to make. By noon, I knew I had no choice but to tell the detectives the truth, regardless of the personal consequences. The stakes were just too high. More lives could be at risk if the killer was not caught soon.

I had some evidence from the larceny that needed turning in, so I marked en route to CHC (central headquarters campus). I placed the evidence in the property section and started walking over to the Homicide Division. En route I saw a young evening-shift patrol officer I had not seen since the murder. Frank had joined the agency only a few months ahead of me.

I smiled and reached out to shake his hand. "Frank, how's life?"

"I'm okay, Tim. . . . Rough morning, though."

"You do look a little frazzled," I offered.

"Tim, you know the E Street Apartments murder . . . the one we saw each other at when I was working day shift overtime?"

"Of course, what's up?" Even talking in the hall casually about the murder was difficult.

"I was working out at the fire department early this morning when the day shift guy came in after your roll call. He told me about the sergeant's comments and the two hair strands."

"What's that got to do with you? If memory serves, you were the guy at the front door making sure no one came into the apartment. You were never near that bedroom."

"You mean, I *shouldn't* have been near that bedroom. But yeah, I went in the room. It was just a few seconds when I first got there, and there was all sorts of commotion going on with the screaming family.

I didn't tell anyone because I didn't think it was a big deal. I basically just walked in and walked out. But crap, Tim, was it ever a big deal. Thinking that hair might be mine, I came straight in from the fire department."

"So, what happened when you got here?" Now, I was really feeling tortured. It had taken me hours to come to a decision that Frank had made in seconds. And what if it was Frank's hair and not mine? Could I be so lucky?

"Tim, Forensics took a hair from my head and examined it against the white guy's hair strand from the room. They were identical. All is well, and the investigation is back on track. Now I just need to wait and see what will happen to me."

## Discussion Questions

1.  What other possible considerations and consequences could Officer Vaughn have taken into account in his decision-making process?

2.  We all grew up being told not to tell even small lies because one small lie almost always spirals into more and often bigger lies. With this thought, where did Officer Vaughn make his real mistake?

3.  Realizing that we never really know what we would do unless something actually happens to us, take a minute to reflect on your personal values. Do you think you would have had the courage and character to come forward immediately like Frank or at least in a few hours like Officer Vaughn?

# Part VI
## Self-Reporting

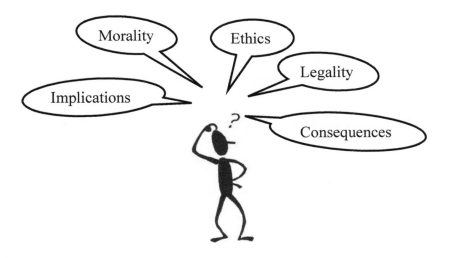

*There is no well-defined boundary line between honesty and dishonesty. The frontiers of one blend with the outside limits of the other, and he who attempts to tread this dangerous ground may be sometimes in one domain and sometimes in the other.*

~ O. Henry

I first saw the Oath of Honor hanging on an office wall at the FBI National Academy. It is well written and concisely captures the sense of who we aspire to be, who we commit to be, in the policing community. What I found particularly interesting was the importance placed on accountability— one-third of the entire oath. *I will always have the courage to hold myself and others accountable for our actions.* Does this wording place an affirmative duty on each of us to report not only the unethical behavior of others but our own as well?

> *On my honor, I will never betray my badge, my integrity, my character, or the public trust.*
>
> *I will always have the courage to hold myself and others accountable for our actions.*
>
> *I will always uphold the constitution and community I serve.*
> ~ Law Enforcement Oath of Honor

Little is written in the law enforcement literature about the ethics of self-reporting misconduct, mistakes, and abuses. Perhaps this is too much to ask of our police. Perhaps it is exactly what we should require of our officers. What was evident in writing this book was that several of the ethical dilemmas from my past, as well as stories from my colleagues and from our students, surrounded this very issue.

# 18

# The Day Planner

*Action, indeed, is the sole medium of expression for ethics.*

~ Jane Addams

## Detective Cheryl Barnes's Story

You may often hear that being a woman in law enforcement has its share of difficulties. Sure, there are guys who think women are too physically weak or emotionally sensitive. Then there's the home life, where balancing the demands of being a wife, mom, and cop are sometimes almost overwhelming. But women also face some smaller, practical difficulties, such as figuring out where to carry our gun off duty or in plainclothes on duty, especially when we're wearing a dress or skirt.

After many years of trying all kinds of holsters in all sorts of places, I was thrilled when I found the day planner holster. It looks like a day planner on the outside but is designed on the inside to holster a pistol (as well as keep my schedule). And they even come in an assortment of colors and materials. The day planner holster became a mainstay with me for many years.

A couple of years ago, my family and I were out to dinner in a nearby town. As was the case most of the time off duty, my husband (also law enforcement) carried a Glock 27 on his ankle. I carried a Sig Sauer 9mm in my day planner holster. After a great dinner with the family, we headed to the movies.

The night could not have gone better—good food, fun movie, lots of popcorn, and most important, a wonderful evening with my husband and children—until my work cell phone rang.

I almost didn't answer it. I was having such a great family night, without any work stresses. But in my field, I really didn't have a choice.

"Detective Barnes," I answered.

"Detective, this is Amanda at the Country Inn Restaurant. I think you left something very important on the table, a . . . day planner? I had to look through it for identification. I found your business cards, but . . . well, . . ."

"Amanda, thank you so much. I am very sorry. I will be there in thirty minutes at the most."

"I'll keep it safe for you," she offered kindly.

It was horrible enough that I had left a loaded weapon in a public setting, where a small child or anyone could have been hurt. But I had not even realized that my gun was missing. How could this have possibly happened? How could I have been so preoccupied with my evening that I'd left my gun on the table over two hours earlier and not even known it?

And what would the police department do to me? This would be a big deal to the brass. My husband was telling me over and over that everything would be fine. I knew this wasn't the end of the world, but I also knew everything would not be just fine. If they found out, this would result in an official dereliction of duty charge, with a suspension to follow. In my department, this charge was often the kiss of death for an officer's career. And for those few sexist cops I worked with, this would be just one more piece of evidence that women should not be in law enforcement.

I walked through the restaurant door with my mind racing. I immediately saw our waitress just a few steps away.

"Amanda, my name is Cheryl. We spoke on the phone."

"Of course. Here is what you're looking for, Detective. I imagine this sort of thing is frowned upon in your department, so no worries about me saying anything."

You are Detective Cheryl Barnes. Reflect on these questions and considerations before reading the real-life outcome.

1. Do you report the incident to the department and face the consequences?
2. Do you thank Amanda for her discretion and never mention the incident again?
3. Is there some other course of action?

## Considerations

### *Amanda*

- What if Amanda changes her mind and reports you?
- What if Amanda stays true to her word but does tell a friend who reports you?
- Your decision may leave lasting impressions on Amanda and everyone she influences for many years—positive or negative.
- What if Amanda, as kind as she is, ever needs a favor from the police?

### *Your Husband*

- Your husband is a fellow law enforcement officer. Your decision may affect his employment, particularly if you do not self-report and his agency finds out that he knew.
    - Does he have a *legal* or *policy* affirmative obligation to report the incident?
    - A *moral* affirmative obligation?

- Does he feel strongly one way or the other, or is he noncommittal but will support whatever your decision is?

***Personal and Professional Consequences***

- You know that failure to maintain security of your weapon is a serious internal charge. You will be substantively disciplined if you report this incident.
- You know from years on the job that substantiated internal investigation charges like this can be the tie-breaker between candidates in the promotion process for many years to come.
- What would your department heads do if you did not self-report the incident yet they found out anyway? While not an ethical issue, it is a practical one. Knowing the discipline will be much worse for hiding the incident, are you willing to take that chance?
- The bottom line is that no one was harmed, and no one will probably ever find out about the incident. However, you will know even if others do not. Does this matter to you?
- It is tough enough earning the respect of your male peers and bosses. This could harm not only your reputation as a female officer but the reputation of all the women in the department.
- You know you messed up. But the incident taught you a powerful lesson in responsibility. Further embarrassment and discipline by self-reporting may have no real value in this regard.

# The Real-Life Decision

"Yes, Amanda, my department would very much frown on this. I was careless tonight, and I am very sorry. I am also deeply grateful to you."

I was careful in my response to Amanda. I had not made up my mind what to do with the department. I thought my response was vague enough to cover whatever my decision turned out to be.

We went home, tucked the kids into bed, and sat down in the family room.

"Bill, I really, really messed up tonight. I know no one was hurt, but what if a little kid had picked up my day planner and started playing with it?"

"I know, but we all make mistakes. We're all human."

"I hope I'm making the right decision. I learned my lesson tonight. This will never happen again. But tonight was a mistake of the mind, not of the heart. I'm not going to report this."

## Discussion Questions

1.  What do you think Detective Barnes meant by "mistake of the mind" versus "mistake of the heart"?

2.  Was leaving her gun at the table really a big deal anyway? No one was hurt, and the gun was back in her hands that evening. Or do the potential consequences of the action make it a big deal? What if a child had found it? What if it had fallen into the hands of a criminal?

3.  This may be the first and only time Amanda will engage one-on-one with a police officer in her life. Detective Barnes's decision may leave a lasting and perhaps profound impression of the entire law enforcement community. Would this responsibility affect your decision?

4.  Do you agree or disagree with the real-life decision Detective Barnes made? Really think this through and answer as honestly as you can.

5.  Change Detective Barnes's rank to captain. Would that affect your decision? Explain.

# 19
# Karma

*Integrity is telling myself the truth. Honesty is telling the truth to other people.*

~ Spencer Johnson

## Officer Brandon Griffith's Story

I have been a small town cop my entire life. When I started, we had four sworn officers, including the chief. Nearly twenty-five years later, we had grown to only seven patrol officers, one captain, and the chief. I considered many times over the years the idea of moving to the big city—more action, more money, the kind of policing you see on TV. But every time I got close to making the move, the pull of family, friends, church, and knowing everyone in town kept me grounded right where I am today.

I discovered over my career that what I do *is* real policing, just on a smaller scale than the city cops. And I don't think morality and ethics really change that much based on the size of the department. I made a decision many years ago that I still think about today. It wasn't a life or death decision. Most ethical choices in policing are not.

I had been married less than a year, and the marriage had been rocky from day one. We were young and dumb like most newlyweds, but we had another strike against us. We both had tempers that could get ugly behind closed doors. We never put hands on each other in these fights, but it wasn't uncommon for things (flower pots, lamps, chairs. . . .) to going flying through a room. She was more volatile and quicker to anger, but she still could push my buttons faster than anyone I had ever known.

I pulled up in the driveway one evening after work in my take-home police car. It had been a long week, with regular shift work, overtime hours, and court. Maddie was waiting in the driveway with that look in her eyes. I don't remember the details of what started the argument, but it had something to do with me putting in too many hours at work while she had to do everything at home with no help from me.

The argument turned into a screaming match pretty quickly. Then out of nowhere, she grabbed a pipe on the edge of the gravel driveway and swung as hard as she could at my police car. She got three swings on the rear bumper before I got to her and forced the pipe out of her hand. In the process, I also threw her hard against the side of the car.

That was the first time I had ever grabbed Maddie in anger. That moment ended the argument, with her running inside in tears. Both of us had crossed the line. She had bruises on her shoulders, and I had a dented police car. As weird as this may sound, that evening was a turning point for the better in our marriage. We had crossed a point we did not want to cross again.

Setting aside the marital issues, the rear bumper of the police car was smashed. If I reported what really happened, the department would find out about my marital problems and my temper. And if the bruises on my wife's shoulders came into play, I could be out of a job. They might even feel compelled to prosecute me for domestic abuse and my wife for destruction of government property. I could always tell the department I found my car like that when I left the courthouse earlier that afternoon. Or I could not report the incident at all. I could take the car somewhere out of town and get it fixed before my next shift in three days. Whatever the choice, I had to make my decision quickly.

You are Officer Brandon Griffith. Reflect on these questions and considerations before reading the real-life outcome.

1. Do you truthfully report the incident?
2. Do you falsely report the incident?
3. Do you not report the incident at all?

## Considerations

### *Legal and Policy Issues*

- Are there any laws requiring you to report the intentional destruction of government property?
- Do any departmental or local government policies require you to report?
- Did the physical nature of your domestic dispute and the evidence (bruised shoulders) rise to a level at which an officer would have been required to make an arrest?
- If you falsely reported the incident and were caught, would there be legal ramifications? Consider the implications of such cases as *Brady, Giglio,* and *Henthorn.*
- If you reported truthfully, would there be legal implications for you related to domestic abuse?
- If you reported truthfully, would there be legal implications for your wife for the vandalism?

### *Professional Consequences*

- If you truthfully reported the incident, would it negatively affect your career?
- If you falsely reported the incident and were caught, how would that affect your career?
- If you did not report the incident and fixed the car yourself and were caught, would that affect your career?

# The Real-Life Decision

My wife's brother worked for a tow truck company in the city about an hour away. I called him that night and explained what had happened.

Hesitantly, I asked my brother-in-law, "Do you guys work with any body shops up there that would fix this for me at a fair price and do it discreetly?"

"Brandon, get in the car right now and head north. I'll meet you where I work in an hour. I'll take care of everything. Make right with my sister and don't worry about the car. I got it."

This incident happened over fifteen years ago, when I was a young patrol officer. It's funny how I still think about it. But it did not come full circle until last year, when a local body shop (one town over) called me early one morning.

"Captain, this is Johnny Bordeaux. I run an auto glass shop over in Harrison."

"I know the place well, Johnny. We've done some work with you guys over the years. What can I do for you?"

"Well, one of your officers, Bill is his name, dropped off his police car yesterday to get the windshield replaced. He said it was real important that he get it back by today's afternoon shift. Real nice boy, said it was personal, and that he was going to pay for it himself. The reason I'm calling is that I don't have that windshield in stock. I tried calling Bill's cell phone several times but no answer. Can you let him know that it looks like Tuesday is the best I can do?"

## Discussion Questions

1. The considerations to ponder in the previous pages really do not fall within the moral or ethical arena. Taking those consequences and implications off the decision-making plate, what is the *right* thing to do?

2. Now, after considering the many possible implications and reflecting on the moral decision in question 1, what do you think you would do?

# 20
# Monsters Among Us

*Day by day, what you choose, what you think, and what you do is who you become. Your integrity is your destiny.*

~ Heraclitus

## Officer Richard Lowery's Story

A career in law enforcement, as with many first-responder professions, offers a unique view into some of the most extraordinary qualities of humanity. Yet it also provides a dim look into some of its most tragic elements. Years on the job experiencing violence in countless ways, seeing death in so many sad circumstances, and watching seemingly good people do horrible things had indelibly hardened me. Officers often lose a little of themselves through this process, but it is a necessary defense to endure a career protecting and serving our communities. Many years later, I still remember one call that affected me in many ways.

"Bravo 1435, aggravated domestic, Green Castle Trailer Park, number 146."

"Bravo 1435 en route."

I was the first to arrive. On an aggravated domestic, we usually waited for backup, but I decided to approach the residence alone because of yelling from a female inside the trailer. I beat on the door twice, identifying myself loudly each time. There was no response, and the yelling had stopped. I walked around the side of the trailer to see if I could get a glimpse inside. Through a bedroom window, I saw a woman on the floor unconscious.

"Bravo 1435, unconscious female on floor in residence. I'm making entry. Send Rescue."

Neither the front door nor the husband offered any real resistance. As I handcuffed him, my backup arrived. I left him with the arriving officer, and I ran to the bedroom to check on the wife. She was okay. There were no signs of violence or trauma whatsoever.

"Ma'am, did your husband hurt you?"

"Not like you are thinking. He never touched me. When I heard you at the door, all my emotions just crashed on me, and I must have fainted. But I can't live like this anymore."

"What's really going on here?" I asked.

"My three-year-old daughter has been telling me for a few weeks that Bob has been touching her in private places. I never thought too much of it. Bob's her stepfather, so hugging her or giving her baths is normal."

"What happened tonight?"

"When I got home from work, my daughter was hiding in her closet and wouldn't come out. When she finally talked to me, she described some pretty unimaginable things Bob had done." The wife spent the next five minutes telling me word for word what her daughter had said. If this was true, Bob was an animal who needed to spend the rest of his life behind bars.

A third officer who had come to the scene had already checked the rest of the trailer and found the daughter hiding in her room. I spoke to the child just to get some sense that her mom was telling me the truth. After briefly speaking with the daughter, there was no doubt in my mind about the veracity of her story.

I walked back into the family room to the husband cuffed on the ground. The officer who was there went with the paramedics to check on the daughter. The stepfather looked up and said with a gentle voice, "I'd like to leave now. I never touched my wife, so please take these cuffs off so I can go."

I had a decision to make. He had committed no crime in my presence. There was no sign of evidence against the mother. In fact, she had verified as much. I had to let him go or arrest him for the one crime for which I felt probable cause did exist—child abuse.

"No, you are not free to leave. You are under arrest for felony child abuse." I then went on to explain his rights under Miranda. "You have the right to remain silent. Anything you say can be used against you in a court of law. You have the right to speak with an attorney before any questioning. If you cannot afford an attorney, one will be appointed to you if you wish. If you do decide to talk, you can stop talking at any time. Do you understand these rights?"

"I do understand them, Officer. And I want to speak to an attorney before any questioning."

I did not intend to ask him any questions. I just read him his rights because that's what I did when I arrested someone. My focus now was on protecting the child and building a case against the stepfather. But neither was in my lane beyond what I had already done. I called out Child Protective Services and the on-call crimes against juveniles (CJ) detective.

Detective Jennifer Davis arrived within half an hour. She had a way about her. She was hard-core but could charm a confession out of the worst of the bad guys. I explained what the mother had told me as well as the few words the daughter had said. Davis agreed that probable cause existed for the arrest. She thanked me and took the stepfather out to her car and then to headquarters for questioning and processing.

I found out a few days later from Davis that the stepfather had provided a complete confession to her at the office that evening. It was all on tape for the jury to see. There was some corroborating evidence in this case too, but the confession would be the key.

I didn't hear any more about the case until many months later, just a few days before trial, when my phone rang at home.

"Lowery, this is Davis from the CJ unit. F---ing tell me right now that you did not read Miranda rights to the stepfather that night at Green Castle Trailer Park."

"I don't understand, Detective. What's going on?"

"He's telling his attorney that you read him his rights, and that he invoked his right to counsel before I even got there."

"So, what if I did? I didn't ask him a single question."

"Jesus, Lowery, how long have you been a cop? Look, I explained his rights to him at my office that evening, and he waived them. And he confessed! But none of that matters if he had already been given his rights by you and invoked his right to counsel. My whole f---ing confession gets suppressed. Is this making any sense to you? You tell me you did this, and a child-molesting monster goes free!"

You are the Officer Richard Lowery. Reflect on these questions and considerations before reading the real-life outcome.

1. Do you tell the truth?
2. Do you deny it ever happened?
3. Is there some other course of action?

## Considerations

### Legal Issues

- The rights afforded citizens under the Miranda ruling, as interpreted in your jurisdiction, mean no other officer that evening could have legally interviewed the stepfather after he invoked his right to an attorney. The confession would be suppressed.
- Putting a three-year-old victim on the stand to testify about sexual abuse will not happen in your jurisdiction.
- As described in this scenario, the corroborating evidence would not be sufficient to convict the stepfather without the confession.
- If you lie in your testimony, you will be exposing yourself to perjury.

### Moral Issues

- A confessed child molester will go free if you tell the truth.
- Lying to the officer will necessarily lead to having to lie under oath in court (perjury). Are you willing to start down that moral slippery slope?

- If you tell the truth, who knows what other horrible abuses may happen to other children?
- Your testimony will affect the rest of the child's life.

## The Real-Life Decision

"Detective, I did not read or explain to him in any way his Miranda rights. That's a fact, and I will unequivocally testify to that under oath."

"And there were no witnesses to you giving him Miranda?"

"What? I told you. It never happened. There was no one there who can testify they heard me explain Miranda to him. It just didn't happen, and that's it."

"Lowery, what you're missing in intelligence, you more than make up for in character. You're a good man. Thank you."

Detective Davis obviously knew I was lying. Would it be that apparent to the court or defense too? I knew the path I had committed to follow was wrong in the eyes of the law. I would have to jeopardize my reputation with the court. I would have to commit perjury. But I was okay with that. While this would pose a dilemma for many, it didn't for me. I could not let my mistake stand in the way of justice.

It was the day of trial, and the courtroom was bustling with activity before the judge arrived. Nothing unusual about this except that the defense attorney had a look of panic on his face as he scurried around the courtroom, talking on his phone. The judge entered, and the bailiff gave the "all rise" command. It then hit me. The stepfather was nowhere to be found. After consulting with the prosecutor and the defense attorney, the judge revoked his bail and ordered the sheriff's office to bring him in immediately. The court then adjourned for two hours.

About an hour later, Davis called me on my cell phone. "Lowery,

I'm at the apartment this guy has been staying at the past few months. You won't believe this."

"What happened?"

"This piece of scum is hanging from a rope in his closet. He left a full confession in a suicide letter that matched what he told me that evening. He even admitted to other abuses we had no idea about. It looks like we won't be going to trial today."

## Discussion Questions

1. Are there other legal or moral issues to consider? Identify other potential considerations that should have been thought through in making this decision.

2. Are there ever situations in which service to the greater good overrides an officer's obligation to the law? Really think through your response. If so, is this situation one of them? Explain.

# Part VII
# Maintaining Confidences

We were taught as children the importance of being able to keep a secret. We were taught that gossiping and spreading rumors are harmful. We were told that tattling is bad. Yet we were also taught to report drug dealers to the DARE or school resource officer, inform a teacher if someone had a pocket knife or cherry bomb in their locker, and immediately tell our parents if one of our friends was talking about suicide. The art of knowing what to keep private and what to divulge can be just as tough in our adulthood as it was in our youth.

As law enforcement officers, we are exposed to the most personal and sensitive aspects of people's lives. Many of these situations have deep privacy implications—some for legal reasons (privileged relationships, classified intelligence, or statutory laws such as HIPAA) and some for ethical reasons (sensitivities, professional trust, and personal confidences). Police officers see and hear a lot. What they choose to do with that information has profound consequences in their agencies and communities.

> *Privacy involves the basic entitlement of people to decide how much of their property, thoughts, feelings, or personal data to share with others. In this sense, privacy seems essential to ensure human dignity and freedom of self-determination.*
> ~ Gerald Koocher & Patricia Keith-Spiegel

# 21
# The Starfish

*Ethics is knowing the difference between what you have a right to do and what is right to do.*

~ Potter Stewart

## Captain Cliff Ramsey's Story

One of my best detectives in the crimes against juveniles (CJ) unit was retiring in a few weeks. Denise had earned her position in CJ several years ago because of her stellar performance as a homicide detective. In addition to her experience and work ethic, she brought something unique to the unit. CJ desperately needed more females at that time. Frankly, there were just some situations, particularly those involving young girls, where a female detective's presence was better suited.

As the commander over the Investigations Division, I generally did not get involved with personnel movements at the detective ranks, but the CJ unit was different. It was the most sensitive and perhaps most important unit under my command. I met several times with two of my lieutenants to brainstorm the new selection. We briefly considered posting for the job as we did with other detective positions. But we agreed this position needed to be handpicked from within our existing cadre of experienced detectives.

At my request, the lieutenant over the Crimes against Persons Section provided me with three names of detectives he deemed best qualified. All three looked great on paper and had excellent reputations in the department, yet only one was a woman. I have never transferred or promoted an employee based on gender. Any of these three detectives would have been a good fit. But with all things equal, I felt the needs of that unit warranted the selection of the female candidate.

My door was open when Detective Susan Dorsey took a half step in and knocked gently on the wall. "Captain, do you have a few minutes?"

"Of course, Detective. I'm assuming you know about your transfer to CJ. I hope you know how selective we are for that assignment?"

"Yes, sir. And I am appreciative that you offered me the position. But I'd like to discuss it with you. I've never skipped my chain of command before, but I need to talk to you about something personal in regard to this transfer."

"Come in and sit down, Susan. My door is always open." I motioned her to one of two chairs in front of my desk.

Susan closed the door and sat down. "I need to talk with you about why I cannot accept this position. This is extremely personal and cannot leave the room. I've never told anyone, and I don't ever want to talk about it again."

"Feel free to talk to me about anything. But, you know, I'm still a police officer, and I'm still your captain. You can't admit to committing a crime and expect me to maintain that confidence."

"Nothing like that, sir. It's something that happened to me many years ago." Susan wiped her eyes.

"Okay, talk to me."

She spent quite a while talking about problems she was having maintaining relationships with men. She talked about waking up at night because of bad dreams. She talked about having a hard time getting out of bed on weekends. I more or less just listened for about half an hour. I still did not know where this conversation was going, if anywhere at all.

"Susan, obviously I am not an expert in any way on difficulties like you are experiencing, but what you are describing sounds like classic symptoms of depression. Have you considered talking with EAP or a professional outside the department about what's causing these problems?"

"I know exactly what's causing my anxieties and depression. It's the same reason I just can't work in the CJ unit." Susan looked down at the floor for several seconds and then raised her head as the tears flowed. "Captain, my stepfather sexually abused me from the time I was nine years old until I was twelve." Susan was almost inconsolable. "I just can't work in that environment. And sir, you gave me your word you would keep this private. My mother would die. Please, you have to keep your word."

You are Captain Cliff Ramsey. Reflect on these questions and considerations before reading the real-life outcome.

1. Do you maintain the trust she placed in you?
2. Do you open an investigation?
3. Is there some other course of action?

## Considerations

### *Detective Susan Dorsey*
- Susan is the victim in these events and clearly expresses her wish to keep this matter private.
- What impact would reporting this crime have on Susan's relationship with her mother?
- What impact would reporting this crime have on Susan's reputation in the department or the community?
- Given Susan's current emotional status, can she handle the stresses that will occur in the aftermath of reporting these events?
- Given Susan's silence until now and obvious distress, do you trust her competence to make this decision for you?

### *Legal Issues*
- Your legal jeopardy: Most states have laws requiring people in certain occupations (e.g., law enforcement officers, teachers, childcare workers) to report all suspected incidents of child abuse.
- Severity of the crime: In many states, the rape of a child is a capital crime.

- Is there a statute of limitations on this crime?
- With no evidence other than Susan's word, what is the potential for prosecution? For conviction?
- What if Susan refuses to testify or cooperate at all with an investigation?
- What if other evidence existed that could only be obtained through a formal investigation?

***Community Impact***

- What if the stepfather had been a child predator for the past ten, twenty, or more years, with numerous victims afraid to come forward? We know in cases such as this that when the first victim steps forward, others often follow.

***Moral Issues***

- What if the stepfather continues to prey on young girls? Remaining silent puts other young children in jeopardy.

## The Real-Life Decision

"Susan, first things first—don't give the CJ unit another thought. We had two other outstanding detectives on the short list. One of them will do just fine."

"Thank you, sir. I'm really sorry to dump this on you."

"You didn't dump anything on me. I'm here for you, and I want you to feel free to talk to me anytime about this. But I also want you to talk with a professional who is equipped to help you. What you are accusing your stepfather of doing would put him behind bars for the rest of his life if proven. And more important than paying for what he did to you, there may be others in the past, and there may be more in the future that your silence, our silence, would put in his grips."

Susan agreed to confidential counseling, but she remained adamant that she did not want the abuse officially reported. We talked for a solid hour about the consequences of the decision we had to make. Susan considered herself a realist. With no additional evidence, it would be her word against his. Nothing would happen to him. And she did not suspect he was the type of person to prey on others. In her eyes, she had been a victim of opportunity for a deranged man. Last, she truly believed her mother would take the stepfather's side and blame her for the abuse—if her mother would believe her at all.

The cop in me wanted to move forward with an immediate investigation. How could I live with myself if we later found out this man had abused other little girls over the years and continued to do so today? But even with this weighing heavily on me, I knew Susan was probably right that we would not be successful getting to prosecution, much less a conviction.

I gave Susan a few minutes to collect herself while I ran some computer checks and made a phone call. I checked the stepfather's criminal history. I checked the sex offender database. I ran his name through our internal complaints system. Clean all the way around. Last, I called the sergeant who runs the CJ unit and asked him to put together a package of any reported abuse or attempted abuses over the past five years in which the victim did not know the perpetrator.

"Susan, I found nothing in any of the databases, and no criminal history. And I think you are right about the chances of a successful prosecution. But we have to move forward with this. There's too much continuing risk to the community to ignore this any longer. The CJ unit has a full-time assistant district attorney who knows this stuff inside and out. If you're willing, I'll make a lunchtime appointment with him tomorrow to discuss this. I'll be there with you every step of the way, starting tomorrow if you'd like. Will you do that?"

She thought about this for several seconds and replied, "Yes. I'll talk to him."

The next few months were tough on Susan. Counseling turned out to be helpful but difficult. Susan also decided to take my advice and push forward with a full investigation. This was the only way to interrogate him, and this was the only way to identify other potential victims.

The stepfather vehemently denied the abuse and requested an attorney right away. The investigation went public, and no other victims were identified at this point. Susan's mother was in denial just as Susan had predicted. However, as I tell this story, the mother and stepfather are in the midst of a divorce, and the relationship between Susan and her mother has taken a positive turn.

In the end, I avoided having to make the tough decision of whether to break Susan's confidence and open an investigation against her wishes. She made that decision for me. I am not completely sure what my decision would have been otherwise. I place a tremendous value on keeping confidences. Yet I am fairly sure I would have moved forward with the investigation regardless—not because I was required to by law but because the risk to other children was just too great.

Recently, Susan gave me a small starfish with the following story attached. I keep it in my desk drawer as a reminder that standing with your people in times of trouble, even when you do not have to make the tough decisions, can have a profound impact on those who look to you for leadership.

## The Starfish
### Based on the original story by Loren Eiseley

One day a man was walking along the beach when he noticed a boy picking something up and gently throwing it into the ocean.

Approaching the boy, he asked,

"What are you doing, young man?"

The youth replied, "Throwing starfish back into the ocean, sir. The surf is up, and the tide is going out. If I don't throw them back, they will die."

"Son," the man said, "don't you realize there are miles and miles of beach and thousands and thousands of starfish? You can't possibly make a difference!"

After listening politely, the boy bent down, picked up another starfish, and threw it back into the surf. Then, smiling at the man, he said, "Sir, I made a difference for that one."

## Discussion Questions

1. Identify other potential implications and unintended consequences that should have been considered in making this decision.

2. According to the International Association of Chiefs of Police (IACP), "Whatever a police officer sees, hears, or learns of that is of a confidential nature will be kept secret unless the performance of duty or legal provision requires otherwise." Does this statement offer any guidance in this matter?

3. Police, prosecutors, and judges heavily weigh the wishes of crime victims. Yet crimes may be viewed as acts against the community, against society. Is this a situation where the police need to act regardless of the desires of the victim?

4. Do you believe you would have moved forward with the investigation regardless of the detective's wishes, or do you think you would have maintained the trust she placed in you to keep that conversation private?

# 22
# Don't Judge Me

*When you judge another, you do not define them, you define yourself.*

~Wayne Dyer

## Sergeant Frank Cannon's Story

I had been a road cop for nine years, a detective for six years, and a sergeant for five years. I had seen a lot during those twenty years and met many people. It still baffles me today how seemingly innocuous contacts with people can have such a genuine impact.

Dispatch radioed me about 8:00 p.m. on a Friday. "Unit 41, call communications center—hard line. ASAP, please."

This meant they had something sensitive to discuss that could not be transmitted over the radio. I pulled over to a pay phone (yes, cell phones were available only to the rich and famous back then) and called the center. The supervisor told me that Judge Lenard had just called, requesting I call or respond to his house as soon as feasibly possible. When the supervisor had asked the judge the subject of the call, he'd said, "I'm sorry—it's personal." I got the judge's address and told Dispatch to let him know I was on the way.

The entire way to his house, I kept wondering what in the world a judge could want with me on a personal level. I had been in Judge Lenard's courtroom countless times over the years. He was a great judge—very pro–law enforcement, always protecting the cops from defense attorney propaganda but always fair to the defendants too. Not once in all those years did I have a personal conversation with him.

The judge was waiting for me on his front porch when I arrived. "Sergeant Cannon, thank you for coming. I'm very sorry to bother you. As crazy as this sounds, I didn't know who else to call."

"Sir, what can I do to help?"

"I don't know if you keep up with the personal lives of the judges, but my wife left me last year. All I have now is Linda, my daughter, and she's in college two states away. I don't really have any personal friends. I need to talk to someone I trust, and it has to be in confidence."

"I'm sorry to hear about your wife. And of course, whatever is said here stays here."

"I'm very grateful. Thank you. My daughter called me an hour ago. She's been arrested two states away for possession of cocaine. As you can see, I'm an emotional wreck. Is there any way you would consider going with me tonight to get her?"

"Judge, I'm not sure I can help with the locals down there beyond anything you can do."

"No, no, . . . I don't want you to intervene. You can stay in the car. I just don't want to do this alone."

"Let me call the midnight lieutenant and see if he can get one of his sergeants out early. I'll make up some excuse about something. In the meantime, I'll head home, put on some regular clothes, and let my wife know I'll be getting home tomorrow. I'll pick you up in forty-five minutes."

"You don't have to drive."

"Judge, with all due respect, have you looked in the mirror? You're in no condition to drive. We'll have your daughter out on bail and headed home in a few hours."

I arrived back at Judge Lenard's house an hour later, and we headed south on the interstate. The conversation was pretty light for most of the trip, with a few heavy moments here and there about his wife and daughter. But generally, we were just two guys, who really didn't know each other, passing the time—until we were about ten minutes from the detention center.

"Sergeant, I truly appreciate everything you're doing for me and especially for keeping this matter private."

"I understand family, and I believe in keeping sensitive matters private. Don't give it a second thought."

"If I trusted you with this incident tonight, then I should have trusted you with the rest of the story. I'm an addict and have been for ten years." The tears started flowing. "I'm afraid my daughter is following in her dad's footsteps."

You are Sergeant Frank Cannon. Reflect on these questions and considerations before reading the real-life outcome.

1. Do you maintain the judge's trust and confidence in you by keeping this private?
2. Do you report the judge?
3. Is there some other course of action?

## Considerations

### *Legal Issues*

- How is the judge getting his cocaine? If you do not pursue his involvement with drugs, you also cannot pursue his supplier.
- Has he made deals with criminals or compromised rulings in his courtroom based on his drug use?
- Do you have a legal obligation to report the judge's drug use?
- The judge has not committed any crimes in your presence, and you have not observed drugs in his possession.
- If you report this, what are the legal implications for the judge concerning such issues as his continued employment as a judge or his license to practice law? Should that even matter to you?

### *Personal and Moral Issues*

- You lied to the midnight shift lieutenant about why you needed off in the middle of your shift.
- Can you morally conceal a circuit court judge's addiction to co-

caine, an addiction that could have serious legal implications in his courtroom?

- As a supervisor, you aren't likely to be making arrests and then coming before this particular judge. But if you do, regardless of your decision now, can the judge be unbiased?
- Do you want to be responsible for the destruction of this family if there is hope they can overcome these issues?
- Would you be responsible, or is the judge's fate the result of his own choices?

## The Real-Life Decision

I pulled straight into a McDonald's parking lot. "Judge, I've been around addicts all of my life. I worked undercover for two straight years. You don't look like any addict I've ever met."

He was trying to be strong, but the tears were still coming down his face. His face was replete with guilt and fear. "Sergeant, I'm not hanging out in crack houses, and I'm not using heavy amounts every day. But I use a lot of coke, and I can't stop. It cost me my marriage of thirty-four years to the most wonderful woman in the world."

"As you can imagine, my mind is racing right now with questions and possibilities. First things first, do you have drugs on you right now?"

"No! I wouldn't do that to you or my daughter."

"Okay, we're going to get your daughter and take care of her. I think you'd agree she's priority number one right now. We'll talk about your problems later."

It took hours to get Linda out on bail, and that was with a friendly deputy sheriff and magistrate judge bending over backwards to help. Linda was okay, but tired, upset, and scared. It was good seeing the love between the judge and his daughter even in the midst of this sad situation.

The trip home was surreal. I said little and tried to simply stay out of their conversations. All I could think was, *How did I get into this mess?* I did have one question for Linda as we neared their house.

"Linda, I'm not the cop who arrested you. I want to help you to the extent I can. I need to know your real situation—the honest truth. How bad are you using?"

"Sergeant, I've been smoking weed for years, but I've never done any other drug until last weekend. Tonight was the second time. We were at a party, and one thing led to another. . . ."

"I get it. Look, we're almost to your house. I want you to get a shower and go to bed. I'll come back later this evening to check on you and your dad."

I dropped both of them off and went home. My wife was incredible. She was cutting the grass, a chore I usually do on Saturday mornings. She turned the mower off and walked over to give me a hug and a kiss. She had learned over the years not to pry about my work life. She trusted me, and she knew my motives for keeping work away from home were pure. It certainly wasn't that I couldn't trust her. I just never wanted to burden her with the harsh realities of life that I saw in my line of work.

Today was different. I wanted so badly to confide in her. I really needed to talk this through with someone. But I didn't. Maybe I should have. That's what marriages are about. But I had given my word to the judge, and I saw no pressing exigency to break my promise.

I would never speak of the trip that night, Linda's arrest, or the judge's drug addiction to anyone else. Linda's situation was resolved over the next year with community service and routine drug monitoring. I had gone with the judge to all the hearings and even a few visits. As for the judge, I was able to talk him into getting help from a very private drug abuse center the next state over as well as from a local counselor who had my full trust.

Things seemed to work out okay over the next few years. The judge retired and went back to his old law firm, mostly sealing big retainers on the golf greens. I have no idea, though, if what I did (or didn't do) was right. I can't help but wonder what, if anything, he did in his official capacity over those ten years that was unethical or even illegal because of his addiction. But no turning the clock back now.

## Discussion Questions

1.  The consequences and impact of this incident are many. What other considerations should Sergeant Cannon have considered before making his decision?

2.  Do you agree or disagree with the way Sergeant Cannon handled the incident? Explain.

3.  What might you have done differently?

4.  At what point should you betray the judge's privacy in this matter? For example:
    - When he first told you about his daughter?

    - When he first told you about his addiction?

    - If he had cocaine on him in the car?

    - If he had cocaine in his house?

    - Never?

# 23

# Something You Should Know

*Let today be a day to trust your own inner guidance; a day to have faith that your steps are carrying you in the direction you desire; a day to keep your eyes on the heavens and believe that your feet will carry you well.*

~ Jonathan Lockwood Huie

## Assistant Special Agent in Charge (ASAC) William Alverado's Story

As the ASAC over the district attorney's Office of Special Investigations (OSI), I tended to be the focal point for multi-jurisdictional investigations in the metro area at the local and state level. Recently, there had been a significant uptick in drug trafficking and related crimes. The district attorney (DA) wanted me to corral the resources of state, local, and federal authorities to focus on interdicting the massive amounts of drugs being smuggled into our city. The DA and my special agent in charge (SAC) gave me free rein in determining which agencies to recruit for this new task force. The police department would be my first pick, and Tom would be my first selection.

Tom was a veteran detective I'd met over fifteen years ago when we'd attended a Title III course together. We had stayed in touch over the years through a few big cases and had even crossed paths socially on several occasions. His expertise and work ethic had made him a star within the police department.

I also recruited various other agencies to build the task force, including the U.S. Postal Service. The task force members worked as a team but also had individual responsibilities based on their home agency's mission and jurisdiction. One of the arrangements we had, for example, was that the Postal Service would call our task force when they found drugs in the mail that were under their federal threshold for prosecution. As the local police representative on our task force, Tom would be responsible for seizing the drugs. Sometimes, Tom would simply put the evidence in storage for disposal. Other times, if the evidence was strong enough, he would spin the seizure into a full task force investigation. This arrangement, as well as many others, made our task force the most successful interdiction team in the state.

One afternoon, the DA called me directly and asked that I come straight to his office. When I arrived, my SAC, the city police chief, and two other men in suits were already there. The DA began introductions quickly and concisely. "Bill, you know the chief, of course. And these gentlemen are from the FBI. I've just had a very enlightening conversation with them for the past hour. There's something you should know." The DA motioned for me to sit down. I unbuttoned my suit jacket and sat on the leather sofa beside my SAC without saying a word.

The SAC of the local FBI office spoke first. "We've been watching your task force for quite some time. We're at the point now where—"

I cut him off mid-sentence. "You've been doing what?"

The SAC began again. "About six months ago, one of our long-time informants said a city detective named Tom was playing both sides of the fence. He was skimming money and drugs from seizures. He'd keep the money for himself and sell the drugs on the street through a child-hood friend who 'owns' one of the street corners on the south side. It took us a while to identify Tom and confirm in our minds the veracity of the informant's information."

"And I'm assuming by me being here, you're saying your Tom is the same Tom on my task force? And you're just telling me this now?!" I was enraged at this point.

The FBI agent who had not spoken interjected. "What would you have done in our shoes? We received information from a very reliable informant on one of your guys. We had to develop at least some level of confidence that you and the other members of the task force were not involved."

"I hope you're convinced, and I hope you have more evidence on Tom than the word of a snitch. You guys are on a fishing expedition and don't care if you ruin a good cop's reputation in the process. I won't be a part of this in any way."

The DA inserted himself. "It is the same Tom, and yes, they do have evidence. But they need more. I don't want you to do anything but keep quiet and act normal. This will be over in a few weeks."

You are Assistant Special Agent in Charge William Alverado. Reflect on these questions and considerations before reading the real-life outcome.

1. Do you do as you were told and maintain the status quo with Tom for the duration of the FBI investigation?
2. Do you reveal the investigation to Tom? You believe Tom is being set up by a dishonest informant and overzealous FBI.
3. Is there some other course of action?

## Considerations

### *Legal and Policy Issues*

- Revealing the investigation to Tom would most certainly violate your department policy.
- Revealing the investigation would be viewed by agents and prosecutors as obstruction of justice, a crime that carries significant penalties (Title 18 USC 1503 is a felony offense for which the sentence can be ten years' imprisonment).
- Is there a federal grand jury convened in this investigation? Rule 6(e) of the Federal Rules for Criminal Procedure states: "Any person to whom disclosure is made . . . shall not disclose matters occurring before the grand jury, except as otherwise provided for in these rules."

### *Tom*

- Tom is a lifelong resident of the city with an exceptional reputation in the metro law enforcement community.

- He has personal credibility and trust with you. He's never given you any reason to suspect his integrity or loyalty to the badge.
- He appears to live within his means.
- If Tom is innocent, won't the justice system to prove that?
- Yet you know from recent high-profile prison releases based on new DNA testing that innocent people have been convicted in the past—our justice system is not perfect.
- The investigation could ruin his reputation and career even if he is innocent.

### *Personal and Professional Consequences*

- Is it your place to interfere in any way with an ongoing investigation?
- Doing so could jeopardize your career and put you in prison, regardless of his innocence or guilt.
- Are your motives pure in wanting to tell Tom about the investigation? Consider the influence of your
    - Self-interest
    - Career aspirations
    - Convenience

### *Community Impact*

- If Tom is innocent but the investigation destroys his career anyway, the community could lose one of its finest officers.
- If Tom is guilty and your warning helps him to evade investigators, he will likely continue to harm the community.

## The Real-Life Decision

I wanted to tell Tom with every morsel of my being. This investigation was wrong, and he should know about it. But just as I felt a responsibility and loyalty to Tom, I also felt that same sense of fidelity to the rule of law and the justice system. That night I weighed every potential consideration I could imagine—all the possibilities if I told Tom, and all the possibilities if I didn't. The easy decision would be to keep quiet and let the investigation work itself out. But leaders have to lead; they have to do the right thing. What was the right thing to do here?

I chose to keep quiet. Things continued as usual with my team. Professional and personal relationships did not alter. I had dinner at Tom's house a few times, and we even played basketball one afternoon while under surveillance. We drank beer off duty on occasion, and my wife and his wife hung out together even without us.

The charade was killing me, though. I had worked undercover at various times in my career, but nothing could touch this. And weeks turned into months. I was provided periodic updates from the FBI, but only in general terms . . . until one morning at about 4:30.

The phone rang at my house. It was my SAC. "Bill, I just thought you should know that the FBI, state police, and city PD are serving arrest and search warrants on Tom in two hours. It's bad, real bad. Tom has betrayed us all on so many levels."

Tom was arrested and convicted on multiple state and federal crimes, from drug distribution to murder-for-hire. Even with his guilty pleas and pretrial bargaining, he will most likely spend the rest of his life in prison. And to think, I almost betrayed the trust my DA and the FBI placed in me. Thank God I chose loyalty to the badge over loyalty to the person wearing it.

## Discussion Questions

1. Do you agree or disagree with the real-life decision? Explain your response, and if you disagree, what might you have done differently?

2. An old saying is, "Ethics and leadership are two sides of the same coin." In this spirit, does ASAC Alverado have any accountability in allowing Tom's crimes to occur?

   - Where were the proper controls and processes?
   - Where was the supervisory oversight?
   - Where was the culture of honesty and integrity that is ultimately the responsibility of the leader?

# Part VIII
## Discretion

good**biases**

# decision

*judgment* wants

scrutiny options people

*perceptions*needs *responsibility*

process timing context

trustbadexperience

Discretion is the ability to choose a course of action among various possibilities. This ability to exercise personal judgment, experience, and critical thinking is a hallmark of any profession. Yet discretion is of particular interest and importance in law enforcement because of the police officer's special role in society.

Laws and policies do not address every possible situation an officer may encounter. Many situations are unique in some way and require unique responses. Society needs officers to possess the latitude to employ the correct course of action depending on the special needs of the situation. Allowing context to inform ethical decision making is an essential component of successful policing.

Discretion also presents many challenges, such as the potential for bias, inconsistencies, and inappropriate under- or over-enforcement of laws. For this reason, the police must act within the parameters of precedent, policies, laws, internal accountability, and societal scrutiny.

Police discretion is employed across a broad variety of circumstances. Domestic disturbances provide a rich area in which officers are required to exercise judgment. Officers may determine one disturbance to be a private matter and another one public. The level of cooperativeness of the victim plays a role in the decision, along with realistically assessing the outcome. For example, would the arrest of the breadwinner do more harm than good?

> *Discretion is found both in the action of police officers as well as their lack of action... It would appear to be the single greatest factor influencing police behavior.*
> ~Ernest Nickels

Dealing with special needs populations requires considerable discretion. Law enforcement officers may deal with these citizens as either victims or offenders depending on the unique aspects of the situation.

Scenarios involving the use of force often require immense discretion. While society generally approves of the reasonable use of force by police to carry out their mission, it is sometimes unclear what constitutes reasonableness. Determining what level of force to use may require split-second judgment and reasoning that will be scrutinized after the fact by multiple parties.

Traffic enforcement may be the most visible area in which officers employ discretion for various reasons, such as the severity of the offense or the driver's attitude. Even when traffic offenders run from the police, officers choose whether to pursue based on other considerations, such as the time of day, vehicle and pedestrian traffic, the weather, and overall driving conditions.

These examples represent just a small fraction of the decisions officers make each day exercising discretion. The stories in this section offer a glimpse into police discretion in some perhaps less-recognizable areas.

# 24

# Through the Eyes of a Child

*Look into my eyes and hear what I'm not saying, for my eyes speak louder than my voice ever will.*

~ Unknown

## Detective Darnel Stokes's Story

One of the toughest calls of discretion in my career was not a high-profile investigation. It was not even a large case. It was a simple drawing by a small child. And I knew whatever decision I made would be controversial within our small community.

It was 3:30 in the afternoon, middle of the week, when my sergeant called me at home. Our narcotics squad was scheduled to work that night from 5:00 p.m. until 1:00 or 2:00 a.m. "Darnel, can you come in early today? I need you to run over to Wilkins Elementary School for a situation that's come up."

"Will do, boss. I'll head over there now."

I met with the principal and guidance counselor as soon as I arrived. Earlier in the day, one of the second-grade teachers had asked her class to draw pictures of their families doing something they all do together. Most of the drawings were of mom, dad, and the kids eating dinner or watching television or playing soccer or baseball outside. But one child's drawing was very different.

It was hard to make out exactly what each item on the sheet was, but the overall message was pretty clear. It was mom and dad bent over a mirror on a table with the child watching. The child explained to the teacher that his mom and dad spent a lot of time "sniffing" flour. The child said that the little squares on the mirror were razor blades. He had been told never to touch them because they were sharp and dangerous. When asked what the box in the corner was, he told the teacher it was their television because most of the time he was in the room with them watching TV.

The teacher, principal, guidance counselor, and I all recognized the gravity of the situation. Not only were the parents using cocaine, they were doing it in front of the child, placing this young boy in harm's way. Something clearly had to be done. But what was that something?

The principal offered to go to the house and speak with the parents, but I advised against that for many reasons. We also talked about notifying Child Protective Services (CPS) for an intervention. And of course, I represented the police. Could I ignore, from a police perspective, that I was faced with probable cause of felony drug possession as well as child endangerment? Should I obtain a search warrant for the residence based on the drawing and explanations from the child, which would be in the affidavit for the parents and the public to see? How would this affect the child and family over time? We needed to act, and everyone was looking to me for a decision.

You are Detective Darnel Stokes. Reflect on these questions and considerations before reading the real-life outcome.

1. Do you let the school or CPS intervene and make the decisions?
2. Do you intervene with a law enforcement response?
3. Is there some other course of action?

## Considerations

### The Child

- The child is in specific danger with razor blades lying around the house and broader potential danger with cocaine users and possible addicts as parents.
- Any intervention based on the drawing will have a significant impact, possibly long term, on the child.
- Not intervening will obviously have a significant impact on the child.

### Legal and Policy Issues

- Do internal policies provide guidance in your decision?
- Is there precedent in your agency concerning such matters?
- Does the law in your jurisdiction require you to report this matter to CPS?
- Does the law in your jurisdiction require you to make an enforcement intervention, or is this left to your discretion?

### *Community Impact*

- This is a fairly small community. This situation will undoubtedly become public.
- Although the police shouldn't be trying to win a popularity contest, community support and engagement is important. Will the community want a law enforcement response, or will they consider this a family matter best handled by CPS?

## The Real-Life Decision

"Sergeant, I'm at the school. I've got a unique situation up here. I know what direction I want to go, but I want your concurrence since this is a sensitive issue concerning a young child."

I went on to explain the circumstances. The sergeant agreed with me that both the school and the police were bound by statute to report the situation to CPS. But we disagreed on the police response. My sergeant felt that CPS should run with the matter at this point. I felt we needed to serve a search warrant on the house when the child was at school. The parents were cocaine users and needed to be arrested. And more important, recovering evidence at the house and flipping the parents were necessary in determining who was selling them the cocaine. Intervening in any way was going to affect this family and the child. We might as well do our jobs since CPS would be involved anyway.

"Darnel, get your search warrant. Protect the child as much as you can in the affidavit, and I want the affidavit and warrant sealed for as long as possible. I'll get the team assembled and meet you at the office after you get the warrant."

# Discussion Questions

1. Identify other potential implications and unintended consequences that may have been considered in making this decision.

2. Do you agree with Detective Stokes's position or with the sergeant's original position concerning the correct police response? Why?

3. Is it appropriate to consider the community's response in sensitive circumstances, or should the police make decisions in a completely unbiased and neutral environment?

# 25
# The Turnpike

*Be not too tame neither, but let your own discretion be your tutor: suit the action to the word, the word to the action.*

~William Shakespeare's Hamlet

## Detective Jake Ballard's Story

I got a call at home from my sergeant very early one morning asking me to help with an investigation into a multiple homicide that had occurred overnight. I worked property crimes, so I asked how I could help. He simply wanted all the detectives to hit the street and start pushing on our sources for information.

I got dressed quickly and headed toward the city. There was no immediate crisis, but I didn't want to meander either. As I hit about 80 mph, I saw the trooper sitting in the median strip. The blue and red lights came on. I immediately pulled over.

"Sir, I need to see your license and registration, please. And why the excessive speed this morning?"

"I'm a detective in the city. I was just called in to help out on some homicides that happened overnight."

"Do you have your ID with you? You know, you're putting me in a real bind."

I showed him my badge and credentials. "What bind am I putting you in, Trooper?"

"You're white, and I'm white. And I've already called it in that I stopped a white male. You know what our agency is going through right now—all the lawsuits, the crazy attention in the news. We're getting killed on racial profiling. So now we have to call in everything, and they have people monitoring every stop and citation we write—and don't write. If I don't write you a summons, I'll have to let the next five Latino guys go just to keep my stats where they need to be."

"Trooper, obviously I don't want a ticket. I was in patrol for many, many years and never ticketed a cop. But do what you have to do. No hard feelings."

"If you were in your police car, I could note that in the comments maybe, but I already ran your tags. . . . I don't know. I'll be back in a couple of minutes."

You are the state trooper in this matter. Reflect on these questions and considerations before reading the real-life outcome.

1. Do you write the detective a summons?
2. Do you let him go?
3. Is there some other course of action?

## Considerations

### *Perceptions of Professional Courtesy*
- What would the community or society say about this situation?
- What would fellow troopers say?
- What would your agency say?
- What would the detective's peers say?

### *Legal and Policy Issues*
- Discretion regarding traffic enforcement is a well-known and generally accepted part of policing.

### *Implications of Your Decision*
- What is the possible impact of your decision on:
  - Your career?
  - Your agency?
  - The city police department?
  - Your community?

## The Real-Life Decision

I simply could not believe what was happening. Sure, I wanted the trooper to extend me the same professional courtesy I had shown to so many law enforcement officers over the years. But he was not obligated to do that. So hey, no truly hard feelings if he wrote the ticket. After all, I was speeding down his interstate for no necessary reason. But he was not considering the ticket because I was actually speeding. He wanted to let me go. He was going to write me because I'm white. He more or less said as much. And it wasn't like I could do anything about this reverse discrimination because I really was speeding.

But this was way beyond me. This was evidence of a systemic and deeply troublesome new culture in the state police, of discretion gone awry and reverse discrimination in full force.

His words and actions showed something very clearly. The state police was under immense pressure from every direction—the Department of Justice, the national media, and the citizens in nearly every community in that state—because of a history of racial profiling on the interstate. This young trooper was clearly willing to let minority drivers go with a warning while ticketing every white driver, all in the name of keeping his stats devoid of any appearance of racial profiling. I despise discrimination in any manner, and reverse discrimination is cut from that same cloth.

The trooper walked back to my car. "I've only been a trooper two years, and I'm really at a loss here. But I've decided—"

I cut him off. I could see he was struggling with this. "As far as my situation, I want you to write the ticket. I'm serious. I'm an old-timer, and you're new on the job. Just do it and move on. But son, you've got bigger problems that need to be fixed right now. First, cops don't write cops tickets. You need to think on that. Second, letting minorities off and writing all the white guys is no different from the racial profiling crap you guys have been accused of so much over the years. You've got to get your head on straight if you're going to wear that badge for the next twenty years."

There was a brief pause after my comments. Then the trooper replied, "Detective, I was going to write you a summons. I'm not now. I will issue you a written warning. It means nothing and will somewhat cover my stats. And, for what it's worth, I needed to hear what you just said. Take care and be safe."

## Discussion Questions

1. Most professions extend professional courtesies in various ways. The police culture is no different. Generally speaking, cops don't write cops tickets. I say "generally speaking" because this practice is not completely universal. What are your thoughts concerning the ethics of professional courtesies in law enforcement?

2. Professional courtesy also extends to other activities. If you're in an unfamiliar city and need a ride to the train station, there is a good chance a fellow officer will take you. Or if you need a place to park for a couple of hours at the airport, odds are the airport police will let you park in their area. But at some point, professional courtesy represents an abuse of discretion. Provide examples of a traffic and a criminal scenario showing where that line might be breached.

3. "Professional courtesy begins with the officer being stopped, not with the officer making the stop." What does this mean to you?

4. The undercurrent of this story is discrimination—racial profiling of minorities to make traffic stops and reverse discrimination that unethically disadvantages the majority. What are your thoughts on racial profiling and the solution apparently enacted by the state police in this scenario?

# 26
# Home Life

*There can be no high civility without a deep morality.*
~Ralph Waldo Emerson

## Lieutenant Patrick Sparks's Story

My wife and I did not have the best relationship, but things were okay. We had three incredible children and no real drama beyond the normal marital stuff. Yet I sensed that she had been pulling away from me over the past year. I had nothing tangible to base this feeling on, but we were clearly not as close as we used to be.

My wife's Christmas party had been a nice distraction. I was having a good time, and she was having a great time. I was glad to see the smile on her face. But the kids were home with a babysitter. It was time to get on the road.

Putting on my jacket, I leaned over to my wife. "Since we drove separately anyway, you stay a while, and I'll head home to the kids now. Have fun, be careful, and try not to be too late."

I got home, spent a little time with the kids, and then tucked them in for the night. I walked into my bedroom and threw my wallet and watch on top of the dresser. There was some folded laundry on the stool beside the dresser, so I decided what the heck. For once I would put away our laundry.

I opened the second drawer, where she kept her socks, and put a couple pair in there. Then I saw something plastic sticking out from the mix of socks.

This had to be near the top of the worst sights a narcotics lieutenant could imagine. Buried among my wife's socks was a small plastic baggie of white powder—no doubt it was cocaine. My mind began racing.

How could I have not known? How could I have missed the signs? How could she do this to our family, right under the same roof where our kids slept, where a twenty-year veteran sheriff's deputy lived? Just yesterday, I had given a DARE presentation at my younger daughter's school, where she'd proudly flaunted her *Be Proud of Me, I'm Drug FREE* sticker. As I stood there with more questions than answers, I felt absolute disgust, and I felt betrayal. But this was my family.

You are Lieutenant Patrick Sparks. Reflect on these questions and considerations before reading the real-life outcome.

1. Do you flush the drugs and turn your head? After all, it is your wife.
2. Do you report the incident to the authorities, either your own sheriff's office or a different agency, such as the state police?
3. Is there any other course of action?

## Considerations

### Your Family
- You have been married fourteen years.
- Your wife is the primary caregiver for the children because you work long hours, and she works only part time outside the house.
- She previously worked for a law enforcement agency and understands the devastating effects of narcotics use and the consequences it has on families.
- Reporting your wife would clearly affect both your marriage and your children.

### Professional Consequences
- If you report her, will there be work-related scrutiny put on you? Will you become part of a drug investigation?
- How would reporting her affect your career?
- What would other deputies think if you turned in your own wife?

## The Real-Life Decision

I called my wife and told her to get home immediately.

"What's wrong? Can it wait another hour?" she asked.

"Get home now! I just found something in your dresser." I had about thirty minutes to figure out what to do while she drove home. I knew I was close to being incapable of making a rational decision. I called someone I trusted, someone I had worked with for many years.

"Do what's right for you," he offered. "Doing what's right isn't always easy, but it's *always* right."

"You're not helping at all. Tell me what to do."

"If you flush it, she will own you for the rest of your life. And there will be no evidence, nothing tangible to force her to get help if she's in denial. Yet if you report it, there will be obvious strains on your relationship and lasting implications on her ability to get a job, volunteer at your kid's school, or even attend official functions with you. I just can't make this decision for you."

I sat furious and confused for about five minutes after our call ended. How could she do this to our family? I picked up the phone. "This is Unit 24. Send a patrol unit to my house, please, non-emergency."

My wife arrived before the deputies. She first tried to get in the bedroom to get the crack. I told her the sheriff's department was on the way, and she would have to stay out of the bedroom. I sat her down, hoping she would be upfront and honest.

"It's not mine . . . and why were you looking in my drawers?!"

I suppose she thought I had never heard either of those comments from any one of the hundreds of suspects I had arrested over my career. But I still played along.

"Who does it belong to?"

"You wouldn't believe me if I told you," she said with contempt in her voice. "And you called the cops on your wife!"

"I am the cops!" I yelled. "And you are the wife of a cop who just made a DARE presentation at your daughter's school yesterday. And you are the wife of a cop who is in charge of drug investigations for the entire county!"

I met the deputies at the door and explained what had happened. I led them to the narcotics. The deputies processed the drugs and began interviewing her. It was not surprising when she was less than truthful with them and refused to cooperate, acting as if this was some gesture of nobility.

The deputies asked me, "Lieutenant Sparks, what do you want us to do?"

"Do what you would do in anyone else's house," I replied.

The deputies handcuffed and searched her and then took her to the sheriff's office for processing. I followed them to booking and met with the magistrate to post her bail.

A lot has happened with my family since that night. Not many days go by when I do not struggle with that decision I made many years ago. Many of my fellow deputies agreed with me at the time, but many did not. Yet I had to be true to myself and to my children. How could I profess a drug-free environment to them and condone their own mother's drug use? How could I actively pursue drug dealers yet fail to hold my own wife accountable? How could I get her help when she was in denial that she had a problem? I wonder how things would have been different if I had chosen a different path that night.

## Discussion Questions

1. Are there any other potential consequences of reporting his wife not considered above? Of not reporting her?

2. Would you report your spouse? Explain your position.

3. If you said that you would report, what if you had found the cocaine in your older daughter's bedroom dresser drawer? Would you report her too, or would your ethics change?

# Part IX

## Informants

*It is rarely possible to guess accurately from what corner the informer will emerge. For this reason, a delicate relationship, little understood by the public, exists between law enforcement officials and individual members of the underworld. My attitude has been to use any means available to cut violations to a minimum, and where criminals or addicts will cooperate with us to that end, I will deal with them.*

~Harry J. Anslinger

The use of informants, often insiders willing to assist the police for various reasons, has long been the backbone of successful criminal investigations. Yet the use of informants has just as long been fraught with ethical challenges, both philosophical and practical, as illustrated by any number of news reports:

> *Four narcotics officers in Brooklyn [were] arrested, in a case that involves accusations of paying informants with drugs seized from dealers the informants had pointed them to. The officers are not suspected of making any illegal profit, and official said police officers' trading of drugs for information in the pursuit of arrests could be*

*described as "noble-cause corruption." The practice would, however, shatter police policy, break the law and, in the view of police commanders and prosecutors, erode the integrity of officers. The scandal has led the Brooklyn district attorney's office to seek the dismissal of 150 cases, with more under review.* (Feuer and Baker, 2008)

*Police officer arrested on perjury and official misconduct . . . is facing one count of perjury and three counts of official misconduct after he allegedly lied about his relationship with a woman who acted as a confidential informant. . . . He made false statements about asking [her] to go out on dates, made false statements that caused another officer to falsify an affidavit related to her arrest, and lied about [her] having provided information that led to a drug-related arrest. [The officer] did so in order to prevent the exposure of his personal cell phone records that revealed a relationship.* (Whigham, 2012)

*Two police officers pleaded guilty to manslaughter in the shooting death of a 92-year-old woman during a botched drug raid. . . . [One officer] pleaded guilty to manslaughter, violation of oath, criminal solicitation and making false statements. [The other officer] pleaded guilty to the same four charges and to perjury, which was based on making untrue claims in a warrant [concerning a confidential informant].* (Associated Press, 2007)

Informants are one of law enforcement's most vital investigative weapons in the fight against crime, and their use has been consistently upheld in court (e.g., *U.S. v. Dennis, McCray v. Illinois*). Yet significant discord surrounds their use in our society.

Peter Hermann, a *Baltimore Sun* crime beat reporter, offers some insight into this discord when he describes the world of informants as "a murky, secretive place where cops and crooks mingle and exchange information for money, a place where the line dividing law and disorder often blurs." The use of informants possibly represents the thinnest of lines in our justice system between ethical and unethical behavior. It is obvious from the above excerpts that

> *From the dawn of history, internal law and order has had to depend in greater or less measure on the informer.*
> ~ Edwin Delattre

using informants offers temptations to even the most "noble" officers to stray from an ethical path.

The following chapters continue to address ethical dilemmas from unique perspectives. A recurring theme of this book is that successful ethical decision making requires each of us to identify and evaluate as many contextual issues (e.g., consequences, impact on others, applicable policies and laws) as possible given the time we have to make our choices, then apply the best moral and ethical reasoning we can to our decisions. This is particularly paramount in the informant arena.

The improper use of informants can devastate criminal investigations, set the guilty free, imprison the innocent, destroy an officer's integrity, ruin a department's trust with the community, and put lives in danger. In law enforcement, there is no greater area of ethical concern than the use of informants, no greater moral challenge requiring our constant vigilance.

# 27

# Bring Your Toothbrush

*The best index to a person's character is (a) how he treats people who can't do him any good, and (b) how he treats people who can't fight back.*

~ Abigail van Buren

## Detective Ben Singleton's Story

Over the years, I had arrested hundreds of people for illegal drug trafficking. You can imagine how many court appearances, grand juries, and appeals I had been through—and the equal variety of defense strategies I had seen. One of the most prevalent strategies was to go after the identity and credibility of the informant.

Every once in a while, on very large cases, we would use informants who would actually testify, but that was rare. Most of our informants were "mere tipsters," thus guaranteeing the protection of their identity in court. Yet that never stopped the defense attorneys from trying to discover who they were. On a couple of occasions over the years, a judge had ordered me to identify the informant or the case would be dismissed. We chose both times to dismiss. This case was different.

"Detective Singleton, the defense has offered a convincing case that your informant was a witness in this crime. You will provide his identity at this time to the court and defense," the judge ordered calmly but with conviction.

"Objection, Judge," interjected the prosecutor. "The practice of—"

"Mr. Johnson," the judge barked. "I've made my decision. I want to hear from the detective."

"Your honor," I said, "with all respect to you and your position, you know I can't do what you ask. Informants are the backbone of the law enforcement community, particularly for those of us who work narcotics investigations. If I divulge my informant's identity, my name, as well as every other detective and police officer in this city, will be mud. This would have a devastating effect on our ability to protect this community."

"Detective, I need the identity now, or I will be forced to hold you in contempt and remand you into custody until such time as you do provide the identity of your informant. We have worked together for many years. This is the last thing I want to happen, but I am more than prepared to make that ruling."

The prosecutor stepped in again. "Judge, can we discuss this in chambers, please . . . away from the standing-room-only crowd in here?"

"No, we cannot. This case is different. The informant was a material participant! His identity is not protected."

"In view of your ruling, can I have a fifteen-minute break to discuss this matter further with the detective? Just fifteen minutes, Judge."

"Mr. Johnson, I'm not interested in a plea bargain or even in dismissing the case at this point. I entered an order, and I expect it to be followed. You have your fifteen minutes, but I want the name when we return."

The entire courtroom was quiet as we started walking out. Everyone in there knew this was high stakes. As the judge opened his rear door to leave, and I neared the front exit, he called my name, warning, "Come back with the identity of your informant or bring your toothbrush—fifteen minutes."

You are Detective Ben Singleton. Reflect on these questions and considerations before reading the real-life outcome.

1.  Do you do as ordered by the judge and provide the name of the
    informant?
2.  Do you protect your informant's identity and risk contempt of
    court and jail?
3.  Is there some other course of action?

## Considerations

### The Informant

•   What would happen to the informant if his identity became
    known? What are the possible consequences to him physically,
    to his reputation, his livelihood, his family?

### Legal Issues

•   The prosecutor is on your side, but the law apparently is not.
•   Is there some way to appeal this ruling?

### Personal and Professional Consequences

•   The judge is serious about jail until you release the identity of the
    informant. How would you handle incarceration?
•   How would your family handle your being in jail, particularly if
    the stay is prolonged?
•   The department would want you to protect your informant's
    identity and obey a judge's order, but you can't do both. Which
    side would the brass take?

- Would they support your decision regardless of your choice?
- Will your reputation outside the department be tarnished or enhanced?
- What will be the long-term implications on your career?

***Community Impact***

- The effect on the community would be significant over time. Criminal investigations across the city would suffer as word got out that anonymity could not be guaranteed for confidential informants.

## The Real-Life Decision

I was not new to this business, but I was new to the threat of jail. I was in a real quandary. There was no way I could give up my informant. Word would spread across the city. I might as well go back to uniformed operations because I would never get another informant. In fact, if I gave up my informant's identity, every detective in the city and surrounding counties would pay a similar price. And more important, the people we put in jail for drug distribution are not kind to informants, to say the least. My guy—even his family—could be seriously hurt or killed. But I was facing jail . . . indefinitely. There had to be a way out of this.

The prosecutor and I walked outside, away from everyone.

"Look, I'm going to make some quick calls to some influential people right now, starting with the district attorney. Give me ten minutes. But if I don't get anywhere, I need you to give up that informant's name. This judge isn't playing games." The prosecutor walked about fifteen feet away and began making calls from his cell phone.

A familiar car pulled up abruptly in the parking lot. Then a friendly face was headed quickly my way.

"Lieutenant, what are you doing here?" I asked.

"I got a call a few minutes ago that things were going south fast in there. Are you okay?" My lieutenant was a hard-charging, no-nonsense guy, but he always looked out for his troops.

"I'm fine. I am in a bad situation, though. Any advice?"

"Look, Ben, I just talked to the chief on the phone while I was driving over here. He says this is your decision to make. But if you are leaning toward giving up your informant, you need to consider the consequences this will have on the department's ability to carry out its mission. I agree with the chief on this, but either way, the department will support you."

"LT, you and the chief can relax. I'm not giving up my informant. But you guys have to keep me out of jail." I glanced at the prosecutor, who was still on the phone. "Or at least get me out sooner as opposed to later."

The lieutenant and I began making arrangements for my incarceration. He was very supportive. I could tell he admired my courage, even though I was directly disobeying a circuit court judge. He loosely mapped out a plan for my squad mates to take care of my family regardless of how long I was inside— babysitting, mowing the lawn, . . . he had it all covered.

The prosecutor walked over, but I cut him off before he could speak. "Kevin, I'm not giving up my informant. Just get me out as soon as you can."

The prosecutor held up his hand, smiling. "Let me talk. The district attorney just had a conference call with this judge and the senior circuit judge. We're going to dismiss the charges, and all is forgotten. I knew you were not willing to give up your informant's identity, so the defendant was going free anyway. We win some and lose some. Today we lost. But it could have been worse. Go home, Ben."

## Discussion Questions

1. Journalist Jack Landau once said that if reporters "violate their promises of confidentiality, they may never again be able to operate effectively, except to cover news which is offered by government handout or is a matter of public record." Do you believe this quote to be accurate, and if so, does this logic pertain to the law enforcement community?

2. It may be fair to say that the overwhelming amount of information police receive about criminal activity comes from insiders who would not provide such information if their identity could not be protected. From an ethical standpoint, should law enforcement be able to protect the identity of informants, or should defendants have access to the identity of those who offered information toward their arrest?

3. Which is more important to society, protecting the informant's identity or prosecuting the defendant?

# 28

# The Confidential and Un(Reliable) Informant

*The court, when considering information from an informant, does not solely have to rely upon the "two-pronged test" of Aguilar v. Texas. The court should take into consideration the totality of the circumstances and make a common sense decision on whether probable cause exists for the warrant.*

~ Illinois v. Gates

## Detective Charles Gilmore's Story

Donny and I had been on a roll for the past couple of years. We had just won the Metropolitan Narcotics Detective of the Year award based on the sheer number of felony arrests and convictions under our belts. It seemed like every night we were hitting drug houses with search warrants. We were hard chargers, but our success was mostly due to great informants. And without a doubt, Ogre was our best.

I had met Ogre a few years back, when my new partner, Donny, reluctantly introduced me to him. Donny was fiercely protective of Ogre's identity and kept his true name confidential from not only the courts but the rest of the unit as well. Ogre was that good, providing such a high level of insider information that Donny would not risk compromising him in any way. Donny would even have cases dismissed if it looked like the defense was getting too persuasive in convincing a judge to seek Ogre's true identity.

Ogre was responsible for more warrants, seizures, arrests, and convictions over the past two years than all our other informants combined. He wasn't working off charges either, which meant Donny and I were planning on keeping him around a long time.

The deal with Ogre was simple. He would reach out to Donny or me when he found himself in a position to provide actionable information, if he felt it would not burn his status as a police informant. We would throw some money his way if it worked out. We generally tried to avoid initiating contact with Ogre because we were sensitive about burning him out or compromising his identity in the drug community. Slow and steady but productive was our long-term strategy with Ogre.

His true identifying information was locked in a safe that only the narcotics lieutenant, chief of police, and director of public safety could access. Only the lieutenant, Donny, and I knew Ogre's real name and what he looked like. This arrangement was within policy and seemed to provide an adequate check and balance with the three of us in the know.

As usual with Ogre, he called Donny late one evening, at about 11:00 p.m. "I just left 1631 Dixon Street with a group of people. There are a handful of eight balls in the rear bedroom as well as scales, baggies, the works . . . and two pistols are on the dresser."

"So, if we hit the place tonight, you feel good about protecting your identity?" Donny asked.

"Yeah, there were several people with me, and I saw a couple more going in and out just in the short time I was there. I'm good. But you need to hit that place pretty soon . . . and be careful."

Donny met with Ogre and had him point out the house while I

checked our databases. Nothing of real interest, but the house was in a known drug area, and Ogre was the king of reliability. I got the search warrant from the magistrate and assembled the team. We all met with Donny at about 1:00 a.m. in a nearby hardware store parking lot, where he briefed everyone and I made assignments. We executed the warrant in full tactical gear, with a no-knock entry, because of the presence of weapons in the house.

No drugs, no guns, nothing. One male was asleep on the sofa with the television on in the background. What had just happened?

Donny called Ogre and said with a vengeance, "Ogre, what in the hell is going on?"

"Donny, I've never asked anything of you, but I've given you plenty. You guys owed me this one."

"What are you talking about?"

"Yeah, I lied to you. That guy wronged me, and I needed to show him I had people who could make his life miserable."

Donny and I woke up the lieutenant in the middle of the night and laid the whole thing out to him. As you can imagine, a lot happened over the next couple of weeks, politically and legally, with new policies put in place. But I'll focus here on just one piece, the crystal clear directive Donny and I received from the lieutenant.

"Gentlemen, you are never to use Ogre again as an informant in any capacity. Even if he doesn't get prosecuted for this tonight, he's still done with us."

We understood. Things were heated over this, and Ogre had blatantly lied to us. No pushback from Donny or me.

Several months passed. My phone rang at home one Saturday evening. It was Donny.

"Charlie, let me finish talking before you say anything. Ogre just called. He's in *the* warehouse, the one we've been getting information on for a year. Three thousand pounds of pot was just delivered in a tractor trailer, and several smaller vans will be coming over later tonight for distribution around the city. I'm putting surveillance on it, but I want a search warrant when it all goes down."

"Are you out of your mind?" I yelled. "Ogre's credibility is shot! He's morally unreliable, and he's legally unreliable."

Donny wasn't backing down. "Exactly how is he unreliable? He lied once but told the truth fifty times. That's about as reliable as it gets!"

I lowered my voice. "I get the big picture of all the local dealers this dope will hit tonight. I get that we may be able to take down the source of it all too. But Donny, there are all sorts of implications with using Ogre after the stunt he pulled a few months ago. Not to mention, we are under direct orders from the lieutenant not to use him. And the LT is not just our boss; he's a good friend to both of us."

"I know, I know, I know . . . but that last thing with Ogre was personal. This is all business. He's learned his lesson. And we have tons of intelligence on this warehouse. Look, this is it. These breaks just don't come along every day. This is our chance to really do some good in this city. Ogre swears he's on the up-and-up this time, and I believe him."

You are Detective Charles Gilmore. Reflect on these questions and considerations before reading the real-life outcome.

1. Do you go along with Donny?
2. Do you say no but turn the other way and not report it?
3. Do you say no and report it to the lieutenant?
4. Are there other courses of action?

## Considerations

### *Lieutenant*

- Will the lieutenant find out the identity of the informant should you decide to support Donny and proceed with the search warrant? If so, what will he do?
- You respect the lieutenant and consider him a friend. Does this affect your decision?

### *Legal and Policy Issues*

- Would it be illegal to use Ogre's information again, or would you just be disobeying an internal order?
- To establish probable cause for a search warrant at this point, you or Donny will have to testify under oath that the information came from a *reliable* informant. Would you do that? Would this be perjury? Is it worth the risk?
- Under testimony at trial or at the suppression hearing, you would be asked to explain your informant's credibility and reliability. When

the defense attorney asks if your informant has ever done anything to call that reliability into question, how would you respond?

### *Personal and Professional Consequences*

- Using Ogre as a reliable informant could result in one of the largest cash and drug seizures in the city's history, as well as the arrest of multiple drug dealers across the city. This will be seen as a significant win for the department.
- What will the department do should you and Donny proceed and use Ogre as a reliable informant, directly disobeying an order?
- Your peers will know Ogre was the informant. How would they respond to you now and in the future if you use Ogre and don't report it?
- How would they respond if you reported Donny? Would the ramifications be worse?

### *Community Impact*

- Marijuana is a cash crop that supports other criminal enterprises. This marijuana will be distributed to several drug dealers and gangs in the area. Taking the drugs off the street may not make a lasting difference, but it would be a real disruption. And having the potential to target the original source could make a profound difference.
- Consider the impact if the community discovered that the police were using questionable sources for search warrants.

## The Real-Life Decision

"No, Donny, we're not using Ogre as a reliable informant. Set up the surveillance like you're doing, and we'll start the investigation from that point. We have to develop our own probable cause without Ogre. And you or I will still get the LT on board . . . full disclosure all the way around."

Donny acquiesced. "I can live with that, Charlie. I'll reach out to the on-call DA [assistant district attorney] and explain everything about Ogre as well as this new investigation."

The assistant DA and our lieutenant agreed with the plan. We would start the investigation with the surveillance. Ogre's information would not be used to establish any probable cause for stops, arrests, or searches. In fact, because Ogre had lied in the past, there would be full disclosure to any defense teams related to the bust that we had used information from an unreliable informant to point us toward the warehouse that night.

The next few days were a blur, with very little sleep for everyone. In the end, we made several arrests (and subsequent convictions); seized cash, drugs, and cars; and significantly disrupted the drug trade in the city. The source of the marijuana was identified outside the country, and the investigation was turned over to federal authorities, who had better resources and greater jurisdiction.

Ogre kept pushing to help us over the next year, but we kept saying no and eventually stopped taking his calls. There's no way to know what valuable information we are missing even today by not talking with Ogre. Yet we maintained our personal integrity and our department's credibility. We sometimes get caught up thinking good informants make us good detectives. But upholding trust with the community over the long haul is what really makes us good.

## Discussion Questions

1.  In the real-life scenario, Donny agreed to full disclosure and not to use Ogre's information in any probable cause proceedings. What if Donny had taken the position that he was going to use Ogre with or without Charlie's approval? Would he have acquiesced, or would he have reported his partner to the lieutenant? What would you do?

2.  Utilitarianism represents an ethical system that focuses on the greater good. Within this system, the means may justify the ends. Do the means justify the ends in this scenario? Is the use of Ogre as a reliable source, with all its moral, ethical, and legal implications, ethically reasonable because of the just ends—protecting the community from drugs and violence?

3.  The U.S. Supreme Court in *McCray v. Illinois* affirmed, "The informer is a vital part of society's defensive arsenal." The value of informants, however, is often predicated on their unique insider status—a status often achieved through the informant's participation in criminal activity. This chapter dealt with the ethics surrounding the reliability of informants. Identify other potential ethical challenges associated with their use.

# Don't Search Him Too Close

*Apparent inconsistency makes the law look more like a game than a rational system for enforcing justice.*

~ Jerome Skolnick

## Officer Christopher Merritt's Story

I was less than a year out of the academy and was writing my first affidavit for a search warrant to recover stolen property. When I called one of my previous field training officers (FTOs) and explained what I was working, he was supportive but said he'd never obtained a search warrant in fifteen years. He suggested that I call one of the Crimes against Property detectives.

The detective was great. Not only did he not take the investigation from me (which my FTO said would happen), but he offered to walk me through the stages of obtaining and executing a search warrant. Once the warrant was in my hand, we met with his team of detectives to plan the search. They guided me and answered my questions but really let me do the majority of the planning and assignments. I still remember today (over twenty years later) how special I felt that night.

The warrant went as planned, and we recovered a considerable amount of stolen property related to several ongoing investigations.

The target of this investigation offered to work for us as an informant. He knew nothing more about burglaries in the community, but he knew about drugs. I called the narcotics squad for assistance.

The narcotics detective, Martin Roth, offered to help just as the property detective had. We interviewed the new informant for about an hour. Well, Detective Roth interviewed him; I just sat there listening and watching. Then the detective took me aside.

"Son, through your hard work, you've stumbled into something pretty cool here. He's naming names of long-time targets, real bad guys we haven't been able to touch. If I can arrange it, how would you like to work full time with us for a couple of months?"

This was like a dream. Working plainclothes had been my long-term goal from day one in the academy. The detective was able to work it out with my chain of command. The following night, I reported to the narcotics squad wearing blue jeans and a sweatshirt.

Detective Roth was assigned to mentor me. He showed me around the squad, introduced me to the group, and explained some basic housekeeping things. "So, Chris, the first thing we need to do is make your informant reliable."

I had no idea what that meant. "How do we do that?"

"Lots of ways, but the quickest and easiest is a controlled buy. Here's how it works. He tells us about a place selling drugs where he can make a purchase. We'll hopefully be able to corroborate that information from our intelligence database."

"So that's it? He's reliable at that point?"

"Not quite. We meet him near the drug house and search him and his car, verifying that he has no drugs or money on him. Then we give him money and watch him go inside the house and then meet back with us. We search him again, finding only drugs and whatever money is remaining from what we had given him. Now he's reliable because he's done what he says he can do."

"Got it. Let's do it tonight," I said enthusiastically.

We met the new informant and proceeded with a controlled buy. But before he left the parking lot to go to the drug house, he pulled the Detective Roth over to the side. They mumbled quietly for about a minute. Then he got in the car and headed to the house. The detective and I followed together in one car, staying just close enough not to lose sight.

"What was that private conversation about, Detective?"

"It was deal making. You know when you go fishing, you throw the little fish back to focus your day on the big fish?"

"Yeah. . . ."

"This job is like that sometimes. Your informant is an addict. He needs crack to stay in the game, and we need him in the game. When he gets back, he'll have our crack in his right pocket. Get the dope and any leftover money from him and then pat him down. I want you to be able to testify in court that you did search him after retrieving the crack and money. But son, don't search him too close."

You are Officer Christopher Merritt. Reflect on these questions and considerations before reading the real-life outcome.

1. Do you let the informant leave in possession of cocaine?
2. Do you refuse to engage in this behavior?
3. Is there some other course of action?

## Considerations

### *Legal Issues*

- This informant will have personal-use crack cocaine on him, which is a felony. In some states, concealing a felony would make you an accessory to that felony before or after the fact.
- In trials and hearings that are predicated on information from this informant, you will have to testify that you searched the informant after this controlled buy. If pressed for specifics of the search, you will have two choices:
  - ○ Commit perjury by describing a thorough search of the informant, thus jeopardizing your integrity and career and placing yourself at risk for prosecution.
  - ○ Tell the truth and describe the pat down as opposed to a real search, thus jeopardizing not only that investigation but potentially every case he has been involved in since that night.

### *Personal, Professional, and Public Perception*

- Discretion is part of the police culture and generally accepted, to some degree, by the courts and society, but does this include looking the other way for smaller offenses as a means to a larger end?
- Does it include actively engaging in criminal acts, such as essentially buying drugs for informants?
- Is this an accepted part of police culture concerning informants, particularly in the narcotics field?
- What would your specific agency say about this, both the leadership and your peers? The prosecutor's office? The community?

### *Moral Issues*

- Is this practice, whether limited or widespread, in the best interest of society?
- The new informant is a crack addict. Do you have an ethical or moral responsibility to get him help for this addiction? At a minimum, do you have a duty to avoid contributing to his addiction?

## The Real-Life Decision

"The last thing I want to do is rock the boat. Your whole squad has been incredible to me. But I'm not comfortable with this. Not only is he walking away with crack in his pocket, but we bought it for him."

"Son, I don't like it either. You've just got to look at the big picture. We don't do this sort of thing for personal gain or glory or anything like that. We do it to take the big players out of the game. We do it to make the place safer. Slicing off a little piece of our morality is the price we pay to protect and serve."

"I understand. I guess I'll get used to this in time."

## Discussion Questions

1. What other consequences and implications should Officer Merritt have considered before making his decision?

2. The new informant's possession of cocaine could be considered a victimless crime. What are your thoughts?

3. Brian Lieberman, a supervisor of special investigations, argues for holding informants accountable to the law:

   *Because informants may attempt to continue to use and deal drugs and commit other crimes in their neighborhoods while providing intelligence to the police, investigators must make it clear that they will not tolerate any further violations and that informants will be arrested if found continuing to engage in illegal activities.*

   Recognizing the unique value of informants in the criminal justice system, do you agree with Lieberman, even if this means not having the ability to arrest some of your community's major criminals?

4. Inherent in the police world is the discretion to apply the right solution to the right situation. Does this situation represent a place where the police should be able to exercise discretion?

# Afterword

When I was determining what stories would go into this book, a few interesting themes surfaced, which you may have noticed as well. The first observation was that many of these scenarios have multiple ethical challenges occurring at the same time. For example, in "K-9 Probable Cause," the context was shaped not only by the ethics of Search & Seizure but also Maintaining Confidences and Loyalty & Duty. Similarly, "One Extra Hit" could have been framed under Loyalty & Duty just as easily as Use of Force. "Where's the ROI at His Age?" could have been included under Maintaining Confidences, Loyalty & Duty, or Discretion just as easily as under Diversity & Discrimination. This observation clearly punctuates the complexities of ethical decision-making and the need for strong ethics training and personal vigilance throughout our careers.

Also, many of the decisions in the scenarios involved others' conduct, not that of the storyteller. Maybe the explanation for this is simply that people who make unethical decisions do not readily share them with others. Maybe these storytellers have stronger values than other officers, thus informing a more ethical way of life. Or perhaps we tend to judge others with much more scrutiny than we do ourselves.

Another recurring observation across many of the scenarios was that ethical decision-making appeared to be more difficult when the officers were young and lacked seniority. Although this theme seems intuitive, does it suggest that seasoned officers do not encounter ethical dilemmas? Maybe we become more hardened and cynical over time and are not as concerned with what we deem to be trivial ethical issues. Conversely, it may suggest that we become stronger in our self-confidence to step up and do the right thing, even in the face of significant personal consequences. Or perhaps as we grow and mature, what was once a dilemma is no more. Our moral boundaries, our parameters, are firm.

I also noticed that many of the scenarios, including many that did not make it into the book, were about officers who worked in narcotics or vice squads. Perhaps these types of squads face more ethical challenges because they often employ techniques and practices that, though legal, induce societal concerns surrounding the moral boundaries of policing. Or maybe this phenomenon exists because both the appearance of the detectives and the nature of the crimes they investigate are outside normal community oversight and engagement. Regardless of why, officers, detectives, agents, and their agencies clearly must be particularly vigilant about ethical matters in those types of squads and units.

Another recurring observation was the existence of numerous ethical decision points occurring throughout each scenario. I attempted to surface the primary decision point, but many more decisions existed in each story during the subsequent days, weeks, months, or even years. This was clear in "K-9 Probable Cause," where the trooper faced his primary decision point on the side of Interstate 95, but several more important decisions followed as the case progressed.

Perhaps the most interesting theme was that many of the ethical dilemmas ended with a compromised, measured, or simply fortunate solution that ultimately did not require a black-and-white choice by the ostensible decision maker. For example, in "One Black Hair," the officer did not have to make the tough decision in the end. He went through the mental (and emotional) decision-making process, but the situation resolved itself before he had to act. Similarly, in "The Starfish," the captain was able to persuade the detective to report the crime to the prosecutor and open an investigation. Thus, the captain never had to make the tough choice of whether or not to betray the detective's trust. And of course, in "Monsters Among Us," the suspect committed suicide before the officer perjured himself in court.

The lesson here is powerful. We do not always know who the real decision maker will be, and we cannot always control outside influences or the actions of others. What we can do is consistently strive to make ethical decisions within our area of control, lead and influence others toward moral choices, and model the way by living our lives with honesty, decency, and respect.

> *Fostering virtuous behavior*
> *and ethical leadership is a*
> *lifelong process.*
> ~ Edwin Meese III &
> P.J. Ortmeier

# Sources

Albanese, J. A. (2012). *Professional ethics in criminal justice: Being ethical when no one is looking (3rd ed.)*. Upper Saddle River, NJ: Prentice Hall.

Anslinger, H. & Oursler, W. (1961). *The murderers*. New York: Avon Books, pp. 121–122.

Associated Press. (April 26, 2007). "2 plead guilty in Atlanta police shooting death." Retrieved from www.msnbc.msn.com/id/18328267/ns/us_news-crime_and_courts/t/plead-guilty-atlanta-police-shooting-death/

Aubry, A., Jr. (1967). "The value of ethics in the police service." Police, 12(41).

Bryers, B. (2002). Ethics and criminal justice: Some observations on police misconduct. *Crime and Justice International*, 18(68).

Coleman, S. (2003). "When police should say 'NO!' to gratuities." Centre for Applied Philosophy and Public Ethics, Working Paper 2003/6. Charles Sturt University, Australia. Retrieved from www.cappe.edu.au/docs/working-papers/Coleman%202.pdf

Delattre, E. (2006). *Character and cops: Ethics in policing (5th ed.)*. Washington, D.C.: AEI Press.

Feuer, A. & Baker, A. (January 27, 2008). "Officers' arrests put spotlight on police use of informants." New York Times. Retrieved from www.nytimes.com/2008/01/27/nyregion/27informants.html?pagewanted=all&_r=0

Hermann, P. (October 4, 2009). "The murky world of informants." *Baltimore Sun*. Retrieved from http://articles.baltimoresun.com/2009-10-04/news/0910030041_1_informants-fbi-agent-cops-and-crooks

Hunt, J. (1985). "Police accounts of normal force." Urban Life: A *Journal of Ethnographic Research*, 13:315–341.

*Illinois v. Gates* (1983) 462 U.S. 213.

International Association of Chiefs of Police. (1998). *Model Policy on Standards of Conduct*. Retrieved from www.theiacp.org/PoliceServices/ProfessionalAssistance/Ethics/ModelPolicyonStandardsofConduct/tabid/196/Default.aspx

Kania, R. E. (1988). "Should we tell the police to say 'yes' to gratuities?" *Criminal Justice Ethics, 7*(2).

Kant, Immanuel; translated by James W. Ellington [1785] (1993). *Grounding for the Metaphysics of Morals, 3rd ed.* Hackett. p. 30.

Koocher, G. & Keith-Spiegel, P. (2009). "'What should I do?' 38 Ethical dilemmas involving confidentiality." Retrieved from www.continuingedcourses.net/active/courses/course049.php

Lieberman, B. (June 2007). "Ethical issues in the use of confidential informants for narcotic operations." *Police Chief,* 74(6). Retrieved from www.policechiefmagazine.org/magazine/index.cfm?fuseaction=display_arch&article_id=1210&issue_id=62007

*McCray v. Illinois* (1967) 386 U.S. 300, 307.

Meese, E. & Ortmeier, P. J. (2004). *Leadership, ethics, and policing: Challenges for the 21st century.* Upper Saddle River, NJ: Pearson Education.

Nickels, E. "A note on the status of discretion in police research." Public Justice Department, Mahar Hall 446, SUNY Oswego, New York. Retrieved from http://dx.doi.org.library.capella.edu/10.1016/j.jcrimjus.2007.07.009

Northouse, P. (2013). *Leadership: Theory and practice. (6th ed.).* Thousand Oaks, CA: Sage Publications.

Petrocelli, J. (December 20, 2006). "Free cup of coffee?" Retrieved from www.officer.com/article/10250436/free-cup-of-coffee?page=2

Pollock, J. & Becker, R. (November 1996). "Ethics training: Using officers' dilemmas." Retrieved from www2.fbi.gov/publications/leb/1996/nov964.txt

Schafer, J. (May 2002). "Making ethical decisions." *FBI Law Enforcement Bulletin,* 71(5): 14–18.

Kolnick, J. (Summer/Fall 1982). "Deception by police." *Criminal Justice Ethics* 1(2). Retrieved from www.lib.jjay.cuny.edu/cje/html/sample1.html

Steck, J. (2001). "Achieving diversity through marketing." National Executive Institute. Retrieved from www.neiassociates.org/storage/AchievingDiversityThroughMarketing-research.pdf

Thomson. J. (1958). *The ethics of Aristotle: The nicomachean ethics Translated.* Hammondsworth, Middlesex, England: Penguin Books.

Torres, M. *Kantian ethics and policing practices.* Retrieved February 7, 2015, from http://www.academia.edu/5391020/Kantian_Ethics_and_Policing_Practices.

*U.S. v. Dennis* (1950) 183 F. 2d 201.

Whigham, J. (August 15, 2012). "Delray officer arrested on perjury, misconduct charges." Palm Beach Post. Retrieved from www.palmbeachpost.com/news/news/local/delray-officer-arrested-on-perjury-misconduct-char/nRCYq/

# About the Author

*Jeffrey L. Green, PhD*

Dr. Green has served as a police officer and federal agent for over 30 years. During his tenure with the FBI, he served as both the Chief of Leadership Development and Chief of Faculty Affairs at the FBI Academy. Dr. Green earned B.S. and M.S. degrees in Criminal Justice Administration from Virginia Commonwealth University and a Ph.D. in Criminal Justice from Capella University. He serves as an adjunct faculty member with the University of Virginia's School of Continuing and Professional Studies and Capella University's School of Public Service Leadership. Although Dr. Green's research efforts primarily have focused on the relationship between personality and leadership, he has published numerous articles on topics such as ethical leadership, leading change, human development, motivation and inspiration, and leading in a multicultural environment. He also is the author of *Graduate Savvy: Navigating the World of Online Higher Education*.

Dr. Green can be reached at jgreen@glocalpress.com.

CPSIA information can be obtained
at www.ICGtesting.com
Printed in the USA
LVHW02s2323230718
584738LV00001B/9/P

9 780981 711621